Oprah Winfrey
In Her Own Words

Oprah Winfrey

In Her Own Words

EDITED BY
Anjali Becker
and Jeanne Engelmann

A B2 BOOK

AGATE

CHICAGO

Oprah Winfrey: In Her Own Words is in no way authorized, prepared, approved, or endorsed by Oprah Winfrey and is not affiliated with or endorsed by any of her past or present organizations.

Printed in the United States of America

First printed in May 2023

10 9 8 7 6 5 4 3 2 1   23 24 25 26 27

The Library of Congress has cataloged a previous edition of this book as follows:

Names: Winfrey, Oprah author. | Becker, Anjali editor. | Engelmann, Jeanne editor.
Title: Own it : Oprah Winfrey in her own words / edited by Anjali Becker and Jeanne Engelmann.
Description: Chicago : Agate Publishing, 2016.
Identifiers: LCCN 2016036840 (print) | LCCN 2016053690 (ebook) | ISBN 9781572842038 (pbk.) | ISBN 1572842032 (pbk.) | ISBN 9781572847842 (ebook) | ISBN 1572847840 (ebook)
Subjects: LCSH: Winfrey, Oprah--Quotations. | Television personalities--United States--Biography. | Actors--United States--Biography.
Classification: LCC PN1992.4.W56 A3 2016 (print) | LCC PN1992.4.W56 (ebook) | DDC 791.4502/8092 [B] --dc23
LC record available at https://lccn.loc.gov/2016036840

B2 Books is an imprint of Agate Publishing. Agate books are available in bulk at discount prices. For more information, go to agatepublishing.com.

"[The show is] going to do well. And if it doesn't, I will still do well. I will do well, because I am not defined by a show. I think we are defined by the way we treat ourselves and the way we treat other people. It would be wonderful to be acclaimed as this talk show host who's made it, that would be wonderful. But if that doesn't happen, there are other important things in my life."

— OPRAH WINFREY

Contents

Introduction

O N MAY 25, 2011, THE LAST episode of *The Oprah Winfrey Show* aired to an estimated audience of 16.4 million viewers. For its host, the date marked the conclusion of what had been a largely triumphant 25-year run as one of the most successful talk shows in television history. The "Farewell Season" had been filled with flashbacks to favorite moments from previous years, special reunion episodes, a sit-down with President Barack Obama and First Lady Michelle Obama, and a trip to Australia for 300 lucky viewers. The two-part penultimate episode had been filmed in Chicago's United Center in front of a 13,000-strong crowd and featured appearances from Beyoncé, Madonna, Tom Hanks, Maria Shriver, Tom Cruise, and other notable figures.

Despite, or perhaps because of, all the hoopla surrounding the countdown, the final episode itself was a restrained affair. There were no guest interviews. Instead, Oprah spoke from the heart to her audience, thanking them for going on this journey with her. It was a very personal, completely fitting end, reminding viewers just why Oprah has resonated with so many people over the course of her career.

The cultural impact of *The Oprah Winfrey Show* cannot be overstated and even came to have a name: the Oprah Effect. Products mentioned on *The Oprah Winfrey Show* sold out. Books featured on Oprah's Book Club were catapulted to bestseller lists. The show launched the careers of frequent Oprah guests such as Dr. Phil, Dr. Oz, and Rachael Ray, among others. At its peak, *The Oprah Winfrey Show* averaged over 12 million viewers in the United States and was syndicated in 150 countries around the world.

None of this would have been possible with a different host. Oprah Winfrey is a success because she understands how the power of television can be used to connect with an audience in a fundamentally personal way. Her genius laid in recognizing that people, especially women, would respond to someone to whom they could relate, who they believed understood their own lives and empathized with their struggles. Her authenticity and empathy are two reasons why she has consistently been named as one of America's "most admired" women.

Because Oprah took control of *The Oprah Winfrey Show* early on in the show's run, a move that at the time was considered incredibly risky, she was able to reap the financial windfall that came with the show's continued success. Oprah believed wholeheartedly in herself and her ability to understand what the viewing public wanted. The gamble paid off in a major way, turning her into the world's first female Black American billionaire and making the Oprah brand one of the most powerful in media.

Since the show debuted in 1984, Oprah has been named to multiple "most powerful" lists, won Emmy Awards, been nominated for the Academy Award, and was awarded the Presidential Medal of Freedom by President Obama in 2013. However, all of this success stands in sharp contrast to Oprah's notoriously difficult early years. Born out of wedlock to a teenage mother in rural

Mississippi in 1954, Oprah grew up on a farm in extreme poverty with her maternal grandmother. Years later, she would recall watching her grandmother do laundry and thinking to herself, "This will not be my life."

At age six, Oprah joined her mother Vernita in Milwaukee, Wisconsin. The next few years would be rocky: raped at nine and molested for years by relatives and a family friend, she attempted to run away at 13 and by 14 became pregnant. When the baby died shortly after childbirth, Oprah's father, Vernon Winfrey, told her she had been given a second chance at life. She moved in with him in Nashville, Tennessee, where she began to thrive, eventually landing a job at Nashville's WLAC-TV. There, she was both the first Black female anchor and the youngest.

Oprah moved to Baltimore in 1976 to co-anchor the evening news, but she was removed from this position after less than a year on the job. She was still under contract with WJZ, so the station moved her around, finally trying her as the co-host of the talk show *People Are Talking*, which fit her personality much better. Oprah moved to Chicago in 1983 to take over the half-hour morning talk show *AM Chicago*. Within months, *AM Chicago* was outperforming *The Phil Donahue Show*, then Chicago's highest-rated talk show. In 1985, the show was renamed *The Oprah Winfrey Show*. Due to the early success of her show and the recognition she received for her role in Steven Spielberg's *The Color Purple* (1985), Oprah was able to renegotiate her contract and retain the lucrative syndication rights to the show, which went national in 1986. Oprah formed her production company, Harpo, that same year, and in 1988, Harpo took full control of *The Oprah Winfrey*

Show, making Oprah the first woman in history to own her own talk show.

In 1998, she invested in the female-focused Oxygen Network, which floundered and was eventually sold. Later, she said her mistake with Oxygen was not having enough input in the network's direction. In late 2007, David Zaslav, the CEO of Discovery Communications, came to Oprah with the idea of creating her own network. After some persuasion, she committed, contributing her brand (including oprah.com), her time, and her extensive back catalog of shows in exchange for a 50-50 ownership stake with Discovery, with Oprah as chairwoman.

OWN launched in January 2011; it averaged 505,000 viewers the first week (in contrast to the seven million daily viewers for *The Oprah Winfrey Show* at the end of its run). The channel continued to struggle and five months after the launch, OWN announced that Oprah herself would take over as CEO and chief creative officer (in addition to her role as chairwoman) in an effort to right the ship. It was a tough year for OWN, with layoffs as well as a reported loss of $330 million for Discovery Communications. Oprah later told the *Hollywood Reporter*, "I had become so accustomed to succeeding that I no longer even remembered what it was like to fail."

In 2012, OWN struck a deal with writer–producer Tyler Perry to create several original scripted programs, which have consistently drawn OWN's highest average audience numbers and broadened the network's appeal to Black women in particular. Additionally, exclusive, high-profile interviews with disgraced cyclist Lance Armstrong and with the family of deceased singer Whitney Houston drew millions of viewers and reminded the world that Oprah is one of its most prolific interviewers. In July 2013, OWN reported that it had broken even, beating analyst predictions and reversing the tide of negative headlines. The network has since produced successful series such as *Greenleaf, Queen Sugar,* and *Belle Collective*. In December 2020, Oprah sold the majority of her OWN shares, increasing Discovery's stake in the network to 95 percent. She retains her position as CEO as of 2022.

Oprah's lasting contribution to our culture remains. She has indelibly changed the fabric of daytime television and encouraged her viewers to open up about themselves and their struggles. Above all, she inspires her audiences to reach for the lives they want to live—and she leads by example. The Oprah Winfrey Leadership Academy for Girls, which she opened in South Africa in 2007, has helped girls from disadvantaged backgrounds graduate high school and continue on to college. The millions of dollars she donated to victims of the COVID-19 pandemic helped people across the country navigate one of the most challenging periods in recent history. Her work in film and television continues to amplify the voices of those who are often ignored by mainstream media, particularly Black Americans. Oprah's present and future pursuits, like her other triumphs, ultimately depend on Oprah—and the self-reliance, values, and vision on which she has built her empire.

Previous books in this series referred to the subjects by their last names, following journalistic standards, but Oprah's brand is so synonymous with her first name that we will refer to her as such throughout the book. We hope reading Oprah's words helps you find the wisdom and inspiration to live your own best life.

Part 1

STARTING OUT

Childhood and Trauma

ONE OF MY gifts that I've had since I was a little girl, growing up in Mississippi, being raised on a tiny, little acre farm with my grandmother, is that I knew how to pay attention. I was a great observer of life.

—**interview at Stanford University, April 20, 2015**

WHEN I WAS four years old, I remember watching my grandmother boiling clothes. . . . We had no running water or electricity. . . . As she would hang the clothes on the line, and take the clothespins out of her pocket and then put a couple in her mouth, she turned to me and said, "Oprah Gail, . . . you better watch me now, 'cause one day you gonna have to learn how to do this for yourself." And a voice inside me, a feeling, I think of it now as a voice because it was so strong, said, "No grandmama, I won't." And I felt, in that moment watching her, that this will not be my life.

—*Oprah's Master Class: The Podcast*, **January 30, 2019**

Family is our first reflection of who we are.

—Facebook, August 7, 2016

I SLEPT WITH my grandmother, and my job was to empty the slop jar every morning. And one night my grandfather came into our room, and he was looming over the bed and my grandmother was saying to him, "You got to get back into bed now, come on, get back in the bed." I thought maybe he was going to kill both of us. I was 4. Scared.

—*New York Times*, **June 11, 1989**

I FEARED [my grandfather]. Always a dark presence. I remember him always throwing things at me or trying to shoo me away with his cane. I lived in absolute terror.

—*New York Times*, **June 11, 1989**

MY MOTHER AND I had a complicated relationship. . . . I spent my early childhood—my first six years—living with my grandmother. I have no memory of my mother during that period. When my grandmother became sick, I was suddenly moved to Milwaukee to live with my mother. This was not a joyful maternal-child reunion. I could feel I was not welcome.

—What Happened to You?, 2021

BECAUSE I DIDN'T know either one, I struggled to develop strong roots or connections with my parents. My mother worked as a maid for fifty dollars a week in Fox Point, on the North Shore of Milwaukee, doing what she could to care for three young children. There was no time for nurturing. I was always trying not to bother her or worry her. My mother felt distant, cold to the needs of this little girl. All of the energy went to keeping her head above water, surviving. I always felt like a burden, an "extra mouth to feed." I rarely remember feeling loved. From as early as I can remember, I knew I was on my own.

—What Happened to You?, 2021

My FATHER HAS been the bridge over troubled water for me since the beginning of my life. Had he not stepped up and taken responsibility for being my father after his and my mother's one-time encounter under an oak tree, I would not be who I am.

—**Facebook, July 18, 2022**

WHEN I WAS growing up, I wanted to live like *Leave It to Beaver.* That was my idea of what a family should be—milk and cookies at home, Mom and Dad together, the whole thing. But I wouldn't have become the evolved human being that I'm still in the process of becoming if I'd had everything at my disposal or had everything I wanted at exactly the moment I thought I wanted it.

—***What Happened to You?*, 2021**

MILLIONS OF PEOPLE were treated just as I was
as children and grew up believing their lives were
of no value.

—What Happened to You?, 2021

THE LONG-TERM IMPACT of being whupped—
then forced to hush and even smile about it—
turned me into a world-class people pleaser for
most of my life. It would not have taken me half
a lifetime to learn to set boundaries and say "no"
with confidence had I been nurtured differently.

—What Happened to You?, 2021

I HAD THE most tumultuous childhood. I was
raped at nine years old and, for years, blamed
myself for being raped. I was molested from 10
to 14, became pregnant when I was 14 years old.
I hid the pregnancy because I was so afraid that
everybody was going to kill me.

—Oprah's Master Class: The Podcast, January 30, 2019

I NEVER FELT any connection whatsoever to the child that I carried or gave birth to. And I later heard that my mother hid me, and what was so odd was that 14 years later I did the same thing. And I know what that means. I know why my mother and I have always had such a disconnection because I understand what it means to carry a life inside you and have no connection to that life inside you, to be ashamed that you are carrying that life inside you. So that really allowed me to have a lot of empathy to people who were born unwanted.

—*Oprah's Master Class: The Podcast*, January 30, 2019

I REMEMBER THE first time I realized that I wasn't the only kid who had been sexually molested. The first time I realized it, I was doing a talk show where somebody was telling their story, and I was like . . . dumbfounded. I didn't know what to do. That is my story. . . . That has happened to someone else? I thought I was the only one.

—*The goop Podcast*, March 7, 2018

Most of the struggles
I endured as a child
resulted in trauma
that would define
many relationships,
interactions, and
decisions in my life. It
took decades of work,
conversations, and
healing to break those
cycles and make peace
with my past.

—Facebook, April 27, 2021

As a survivor of childhood trauma, I know firsthand that healing and hope are possible. . . . It all comes down to how you process your experiences. That determines everything going forward, including how you love and take care of yourself.

—*O, Quarterly*, **Spring 2021**

On November 22, 2018, my mother, Vernita Lee, passed away. I was conflicted about our relationship up until the very end. The truth is, it wasn't until I became successful that my mother started to show more interest in me. I wrestled with the question of how to take care of her. What did I owe the woman who gave me life? The Bible says, "Honor thy father and mother," but what did that actually mean? I decided that one of the ways I could honor her would be to help care for her financially. I always made sure she had everything she needed in order to live a comfortable life, but there was never any real connection. I would say that the audience who watched me on television knew me better than my mother did.

—*What Happened to You?*, **2021**

I'D FORGIVEN MY mother years earlier for not being the mother I needed, but she didn't know that. And in our last moments together, I believe I was able to release her from the shame and the guilt of the past. I came back and I finished the work that needed to be done.

—*What Happened to You?*, 2021
[on her mother's last day]

IT MAKES ME want to weep for all the single parents out there who are doing it every day and breaking their backs, their spirits, and not even able to take care of themselves. It also makes me think of my mother differently. She did the best she could and was often too tired to do any better.

—*What Happened to You?*, 2021

I CAN RELATE to pain because I realize all pain is the same. I can relate to being abandoned, I can relate to having people not care about you, I can relate to all of that. All of that helped me be who I am.

—interview with former Facebook COO
Sheryl Sandberg, October 2, 2011

The Power of Education and Religion

EDUCATION IS WHAT liberated me. The ability to read saved my life. I would have been an entirely different person had I not been taught to read when I was at an early age. My entire life experience, my ability to believe in myself, and even in my darkest moments of sexual abuse and being physically abused and so forth, I knew there was another way. I knew there was a way out. I knew there was another kind of life because I'd read about it.

—**Academy of Achievement, February 21, 1991**

[EDUCATION MATTERS] BECAUSE it's an open door to a real life, and you can't get through this life without it and succeed. It's an open door to discovery and wonder and fascination and figuring out who you are, why you're here, and what you came to do. It's an invitation to life, and it feeds you forever.

—***Variety**, October 6, 2015*

I HAD BEEN in Mississippi, which was an apartheid state when I was born. And so, when I moved to Milwaukee, and had just started kindergarten, I walked in and all these little white kids were doing their ABCs and I said, "I know some big words." And I wrote them all down to my kindergarten teacher. Shadrach, Meshach, Abednego, Nehemiah, Jeremiah. And I got myself out of kindergarten the first day.

—*The Daily Show with Trevor Noah*, **April 17, 2019**
[Shadrach, Meshach, Abednego, Nehemiah, and Jeremiah are names from the Bible]

WHEN YOU EDUCATE a woman, you set her free. Had I not had books and education in Mississippi, I would have believed that's all there was.

—*Fortune*, **April 1, 2002**

IF I WAS born just two years earlier, my entire life would have been different. I was born during the year of *Brown v. Board of Education*. So because of that, I never ever sat a day in a segregated school. Do you know the difference that that made in the way I thought about myself? I never had to listen to or be in an environment where a schoolteacher told me or made me feel in any way inferior.

—*Larry King NOW*, January 4, 2018

I LEARNED THE meaning of excellence in the third grade because I turned in my book report early to my teacher, Mrs. Driver, and she was so impressed with it she told all the other students. They hated me every day afterwards, but it worked wonders with the rest of the teachers.

—*Hollywood Reporter*, November 25, 2007

I KNEW VERY early on in my childhood that if I was going to make it, I was going to have to do it on my own. There was no scaffolding, as you call it, built for me. But over the years, there were some very special teachers who took the time to nurture the potential they recognized in me.

—*What Happened to You?*, 2021

I REMEMBER MY father saying to me, "You can't bring Cs in this house because you are not a C student.... You are an A student. So that's what we expect in this house." It was just so matter of fact. And I knew he was not faking it one bit. I never even tried to bring in a C because I realized that it's just not acceptable.

—**Academy of Achievement, February 21, 1991**

SOMEWHERE DEEP WITHIN me, even when I was a teenager, I always sensed that something bigger was in store for me—but it was never about attaining wealth or celebrity. It was about the process of continually seeking to be better, to challenge myself to pursue excellence on every level.

—*What I Know For Sure*, 2014

[SCHOOL WAS] THE only place I ever really felt loved. And it's the reason why for so many years I wanted to be a teacher, to be able to give to other kids what my teachers had given to me.

—*USA Today*, May 20, 2021

THE BEST THING my grandmother ever did for me was to give me the gift of being excited about learning how to read.

—*The Ellen DeGeneres Show*, October 1, 2019

BOOKS, FOR ME, have always been a way to escape. They were my path to personal freedom. I actually learned to read at the age of three, and once I did, I quickly learned that there was a whole world beyond my grandmother's farm in Mississippi.

—*What Happened to You?*, 2021

FROM THE TIME I was a little girl, books have guided me. They've helped me see and understand the world and myself. I owe a debt of gratitude to all the brilliant authors over the decades who have led me to conclude: There is no best life without books.

—Facebook, September 17, 2021

I STILL REMEMBER the shock of recognition I felt when I first read Maya Angelou's *I Know Why the Caged Bird Sings*—a sensation that remains indelible even now. Though I'd read many other books, until then I'd never seen myself on the page. No protagonist, no narrator, had ever looked like me or talked like me.

—*O, The Oprah Magazine*, May 2020

ONCE MAYA ANGELOU had a party. It was a party for Toni [Morrison] after she received the Nobel Prize, and I went to it. I was surrounded by authors, and I felt like I was 11 years old. I felt like I could not even speak. At one point, somebody said, "Oh, I'd like some more coffee," and I got up to get it. Maya said, "Sit down," and I went: "No, I'll get it. It'd be a treat."

—*New York Times*, December 26, 1999

READING IS LIKE everything else. You're drawn to people who are like yourself.

—*New York Times*, December 26, 1999

WHAT MY GRANDMOTHER gave to me, not having a formal education and not going beyond third grade herself, she gave me Jesus. She taught me how to read as much as she knew how to read. She taught me how to read by reading the Bible and Bible stories. So I literally grew up for the first six years of my life believing that Jesus was my daddy.

—*Oprah's Master Class: The Podcast*, **January 30, 2019**

CHURCH WAS MY life. Baptist Training Union. Every black child in the world who grew up in the church knows about B.T.U. You did Sunday School, you did the morning service, which started at 11 and didn't end until 2:30, you had dinner on the ground in front of the church, and then you'd go back in for the 4 o'clock service.

—*New York Times*, **June 11, 1989**

AT THREE AND a half years old, I was speaking in front of the congregation. The hours I spent in that little white church by the red dirt road certainly formed the spiritual foundation for my life.

—*What Happened to You?*, 2021

IT WAS A very narrow view of God. Well, each person gets God at whatever level they're able to accept. That's why there are all these people— Holy Rollers, Episcopalians, Baptists—who can only accept God as a man with a long white beard and a black book checking off the things you can do. And that's really O.K., that's O.K. if that's as big as God is for you and that keeps you under control. Not everyone can be what we want them to be. You still benefit, but your benefit will be as limited as your vision is.

—*New York Times*, June 11, 1989
[on church in her childhood]

LATER, WHEN I was living in Nashville with my father, I accepted a job as a reporter at a television station in Baltimore. As I was preparing to leave my family and the life I knew, my father's advice to me was "Find a church home." At the time, I thought it was because he wanted to make sure I kept Jesus in my life. Looking back now, though, as we talk about the healing power of relationships, I realize it wasn't just about finding a place of worship—it was about finding a community, and discovering true, lasting connection in a new city.

—*What Happened to You?*, 2021

WHEN I WAS a child, we used the term *weathering.* We didn't have a word for the kind of trauma so many African Americans endured, so we said we "weathered." The church was a big part of how we got through. We weathered together.

—*What Happened to You?*, 2021

I WAS BROUGHT up Christian, I believe in the Christian philosophy, but my true religion is the Golden Rule, which is born of the third law of motion in physics which says that what you put out is coming back all the time. For every action, there is an equal and opposite reaction.

—*The goop Podcast,* **March 7, 2018**

Finding a Career Path

I ALWAYS RECOGNIZED that the life for me and the calling for me was something beyond the expectation that people had in rural Mississippi. So I certainly didn't know that it had a name, or that that name would be talk shows or that [I'd] be in television. I had no idea of that. But I knew that there was something bigger calling me.

—interview with former Facebook COO
Sheryl Sandberg, October 2, 2011

YOU'RE NOT SUPPOSED to have all the answers at 21, 22. Or 25. The 20s are about figuring out what you like—and don't. Your first job likely won't be your dream job.

—*O, The Oprah Magazine*, March 2019

I THINK I had to let go of this notion that I could make everybody happy, that I could please everybody, that I was going to the kind of person that everybody was going to actually like.

—*Making Space with Hoda Kotb*, October 27, 2021

WHEN I FIRST started out . . . I was pretending to be somebody I was not. I was pretending to be Barbara Walters. So I'd go to a news conference, and I was more interested in how I phrased the question and how eloquent the question sounded, as opposed to listening to the answer. Which always happens when you are interested in impressing people instead of doing what you are supposed to be doing.

—**Academy of Achievement, February 21, 1991**

I LEARNED EARLY on what I'm supposed to be doing is not sitting in front of a desk, reading copy, and throwing to the sports guy. That's not what I do well. I know how to imitate that. I know how to create that. I know how to pretend that I am a newsperson, but that's not where my heart lies. And so the idea of preparing and reading the news copy ahead of time really didn't sit well with me.

—*Oprah's Master Class: The Podcast*, **January 30, 2019**

I WAS IN my twenties when I was first challenged, in a big way, to regulate my own stress. I'd taken a job as a reporter and was working hundred-hour weeks. I wanted to be a team player, but I could feel myself becoming increasingly out of sync. . . . When I felt the stress indicators that my body was sending, I ignored them, choosing instead to soothe myself with the drug that was most easily accessible: food. . . . But it would take decades for me to understand how to live within my own rhythms.

—*What Happened to You?*, 2021

HAD I NOT been demoted [from WJZ-TV], I probably would have, for a long time, continued on that path, because my father was like, "They're paying you $25,000? You better keep that job." So I would have stayed for all the wrong reasons instead of taking what looked like a failure in the moment and being demoted.

—*The Daily Show with Trevor Noah*, April 17, 2019

IT WAS THAT failure that led to the talk show. Because they had no place else to put me, they put me on a talk show one morning. And I'm telling you, the hour I interviewed—my very first interview was the Carvel Ice Cream Man and Benny from *All My Children*—I'll never forget it. I came off the air thinking, "This is what I should have been doing," because it was like breathing to me. Like breathing. You just talk. "Be yourself" is really what I had learned to do.

—**Academy of Achievement, February 21, 1991**

STAYING IN BALTIMORE would have been the safe thing to do. But sitting in my boss's office, I knew that if I let him talk me into staying, it would affect the way I felt about myself forever. I would always wonder what could have been. That one choice changed the trajectory of my life.

—*What I Know For Sure*, **2014 (on her decision to leave WJZ-TV to host *AM Chicago*)**

PEOPLE WOULD JUST look at me and say,
"How did she get that job?"

—*Chicago Tribune*, May 20, 2011

I NEVER LIVED with a plan. Every one of my
coworkers had tapes that they kept, résumés that
they were always working on. They cataloged
their stories so they knew where their best
stories were. I had none of that, because I didn't
have a plan. . . . Because I always believed "Do
your best and something will show up."

—*Oprah's Master Class: The Podcast*, February 6, 2019

THE CHALLENGE OF life, I have found, is to build
a résumé that doesn't simply tell a story about
what you want to be, but it's a story about who
you want to be. It's a résumé that doesn't just tell
a story about what you want to accomplish, but
why. A story that's not just a collection of titles
and positions, but a story that's really about
your purpose.

—commencement speech at Harvard University,
May 30, 2013

I DON'T BELIEVE in luck. For me, luck is preparation meeting the moment of opportunity. There is no luck without you being prepared to handle that moment of opportunity.

—*Oprah's Master Class*, March 27, 2011

WHAT'S THE SMARTEST thing to do after learning what makes you tick? Answer: waste zero time getting started on living your best life.

—*O, The Oprah Magazine*, August 2015

YOUR LIFE'S WORK is to find your life's work—and then to exercise the discipline, tenacity and hard work it takes to pursue it.

—*O, The Oprah Magazine*, September 2001

I'VE ALWAYS KNOWN when it was time to move on because that is something you feel inside yourself. That I've grown as much as I can grow here. I'm not going to grow any more here. Life is about growth and change. When you are no longer doing that, that is your whisper.

—*Oprah's Master Class: The Podcast*, February 6, 2019

Part 2

CREATING AN EMPIRE

The Oprah Winfrey Show *and Finding Professional Success*

PEOPLE WILL SAY to 20 million people what they
won't say in their dining rooms.

—*New York Times*, **June 11, 1989**

IF THERE NEVER had been a Phil [Donahue],
there never would have been a me. I can talk
about things now that I never could have talked
about before he came on the air. There's room for
both of us.

—*New York Times*, **February 1, 1988**

I THINK PART of our dysfunction in this country
comes [from a feeling] that everybody else's life
is happier than ours. What the talk shows—ours
and Phil Donahue's and a few others—serve to
show is that, really, we are all more alike than
we are different, and none of us are like June
Cleaver. I think we dismantled a lot of that.

—*Vogue*, **October 1998**

WE BECAME A syndicated show in 1986. So I went in to the bosses and I said, "My team, they need to make more money." And the boss at the time said, "Why? You're all girls." That moment in the office, that was a deciding factor for me. I came back and said, "Look, I want to own my own show, and I want to take the risk of owning my own show," so that I [would] be the one to say who gets what paycheck.

—Makers: Women Who Make America, **February 26, 2013**

I WAS NOT welcome in the building. Other people felt threatened by the *Oprah* show, even though we had our little corner office. We didn't make a lot of noise, but we were not the news. I could feel that from people. So just getting in an elevator with other people in the building felt uncomfortable. I felt I had to be apologetic. I felt I had to make myself smaller in that space. And so when I had the opportunity to, number one, own the show, but most importantly, move to another building, that's why I did it. I just wanted to get out of the building.

—Making Oprah, **November 17, 2016**

The secret of [*The Oprah Winfrey Show*] for 25 years is that people could see themselves in me. All over the world, they could see themselves in me.

—interview at Stanford Graduate School of Business, April 16, 2014

I STARTED THE show as a job, and was very happy to get the job. But it was not long before I understood that there was something else going on here, more than just job satisfaction. Something in me connected with each of you in a way that allowed me to see myself in you, and you in me. I listened and grew, and I know you grew along with me. Sometimes, I was a teacher, and more often, you taught me. It is no coincidence that I always wanted to be a teacher, and I ended up in the world's biggest classroom.

—*The Oprah Winfrey Show*, May 25, 2011

FOR A LONG time, I thought it was just a job. . . . [It was] around '88 or '89 that I started to see, oh this is bigger than television, that it's actually a platform.

—interview with former LinkedIn CEO Jeff Weiner, October 15, 2015

IT WAS ACTUALLY a show that I was doing with skinheads and white supremacists where I thought I was showing the world their vitriol and letting the world see that. And I recognize they were actually using me, they were using that platform, because I at the time did not understand how powerful the platform was. So when I figured that out, I literally said, "I'm only going to use my work, this platform, as a force for good. I will cause no harm."

—*The Daily Show with Trevor Noah*, **April 17, 2019**

I LITERALLY HAD a big meeting with all my producers and I said, "We are now going to become an intentional television show. . . . We are only going to do shows that come from a motivation that we're going to show people the best of themselves. . . . But the idea behind it—the vision—is that we are going to be a force for good, and that is going to be our intention."

—**interview with former LinkedIn CEO Jeff Weiner, October 15, 2015**

THE GREATEST THING about what I do, for me, is that I'm in a position to change people's lives. It is the most incredible platform for influence that you could imagine, and it's something that I hold in great esteem and take full responsibility for.

—**Academy of Achievement, February 21, 1991**

ONE OF THE most rewarding experiences for me for the show is opening that world [of reading] to people. I can't even imagine being 40 years old and never having read a book, but there were people who hadn't.

—**interview with Barbara Walters, December 9, 2010**

THE THING THAT sold me was the chance to meet authors.

—*New York Times*, **December 26, 1999**
[on starting Oprah's Book Club]

I DON'T DO anything *just* for ratings, but as I've said, we're in the television business. If you all are not watching this, if this does not attract your attention, then that means we have not succeeded in doing what we're supposed to do as a business. So am I looking for people I am interested in and also that I believe the public is interested in, our viewers? Of course. And does that equal ratings? I hope so.

—*Oprah Builds a Network*, July 15, 2012

WE WERE LIVING it and doing it and being a part of all the experiences we were showing. Girls in the office were looking for men so we did a show about how to find a good man. One of the producers had AIDS so we started doing shows about that. We didn't have a finger on the pulse, we *were* the pulse.

—*New York Times*, May 24, 2011

THE REASON WE were number one for all those years is because we worked harder than everybody else, and we were our number one competition. In the earlier years, every time somebody else would start a show, I would go, "Oh, Geraldo Rivera has a show, oh, Ricki Lake has a show, what are we gonna do?" And I soon learned that I was, and we were, our greatest competition.

—interview with former Facebook COO
Sheryl Sandberg, October 2, 2011

WHAT WE ARE trying to tackle in this one hour is what I think is the root of all the problems in the world—lack of self-esteem is what causes war because people who really love themselves don't go out and try to fight other people.... It's the root of all the problems.

—*New York Times,* June 11, 1989

SOME DAYS PEOPLE just want to be entertained and laugh. You can do a lot of healing with humor. You can have a lot of insight with humor. None of it works if you're not entertaining people.

—*Chicago Tribune*, November 23, 1998

I ALWAYS UNDERSTOOD that there really was no difference between me and [my] audience.... At the core of what really matters, we are the same. And you know how I know that? Because all of us are seeking the same thing.... Everybody wants to fulfill the highest, truest expression of yourself as a human being.

—interview at Stanford Graduate School of Business, April 16, 2014

I THINK WHAT we're all ultimately seeking, even when we don't know it, when I would ask people on the show for years, "What do you want?" everybody would say that they want happiness. But aren't we all ultimately seeking freedom?

—*The Wisdom of Sundays*, 2017

My whole career
has been based
on being truthful
in the moment.
And if I have
to pretend to
be interested
in something
that I'm not
interested in,
it doesn't work.

—*Hollywood Reporter*, November 25, 2007

OVER THE YEARS I've interviewed thousands
of people—most of them women—and I would
say that the root of every dysfunction I've
ever encountered, every problem, has been
[from] some sense of a lacking of self-value
or self-worth.

— interview with Michelle Obama, June 14, 2016

EVEN DURING *The Oprah Winfrey Show* years,
I always felt a hunger from the audience, a
deep desire to nourish not only their mind
and body but also to create a more meaningful,
authentic life.

—*The Wisdom of Sundays*, 2017

THIS IS WHAT I feel is the key to developing
talent. . . . You have to find the thread of
authenticity. You have to find what is real.
That's the key.

—interview with Barbara Walters, December 9, 2010

YOU CAN'T CALL in sick; you can't ever give less than 100 percent. And if you are sick, which I have been a couple times, that's when you gotta pull up to 110, 120. Because people have come from all over the country and this is their moment. They've saved their money, they've bought their airline tickets, they've got new outfits, they've called their sisters, their cousins, their aunts, their mother-in-laws, their mothers, and that is why they're there, to see [me]. So I feel a sense of responsibility, a sense of obligation, a sense of respect, reverence, and honor for those people.

—**interview with Barbara Walters, December 9, 2010**

EVERY DAY THAT I stood here [on this stage], I knew that this was exactly where I was supposed to be. And there was many a day . . . like so many of you, I came to work bone tired. . . . But I showed up because I knew that you were waiting. You were waiting for whatever we had to offer. And that is why I never missed a day, in 25 years, because you were here.

—*The Oprah Winfrey Show*, **May 25, 2011**

I THINK OVER the years people, because of the *Oprah* show and watching me every day with the audience, there is this misconception that I am a hugely extroverted person, but I really am not. . . . If there's a party, I'm the person who's in the corner usually by the shrimp bar.

—*People*, **April 26, 2022**

MY REAL CONTRIBUTION—the reason why I'm here—is to help connect people to themselves and the higher ideas of consciousness. . . . So my television platform was to help raise consciousness.

—**interview at Stanford Graduate School of Business, April 16, 2014**

PEOPLE TELL ME the reason they stay here is because of . . . me. And also because of the mission. A vast majority of the people understands that we're not just doing television and haven't been for quite some time. And a vast majority of the people [are] here because of the principles by which we do television.

—*Hollywood Reporter*, November 25, 2007

I KNEW IT was time to leave the [*Oprah Winfrey*] show when people who had come to the show, then they had children, and their children were now having children watching the show.

—*The Daily Show with Trevor Noah*, April 17, 2019

WHEN [MY PRODUCERS] called me in and said, "I know, we could take the audience to outer space," I knew it was time to go.

—*Hollywood Reporter*, December 11, 2013

I WOULD PROBABLY have ended my show and then tried to start a network. Because what I did was try to do both at the same time. So if I had it to do over, I would end that show, take a break, [and] figure out what the next move is.

—*The Ellen DeGeneres Show*, October 1, 2019

IN EVERY JOB I've taken and every city in which I've lived, I have known that it's time to move on when I've grown as much as I can.

—*What I Know For Sure*, 2014

WHAT I WANT you to know as this show ends [is that] each one of you has your own platform. Do not let the trappings here fool you. Mine is a stage in a studio; yours is wherever you are, with your own reach. However small or however large that reach is, maybe it's 20 people, maybe it's 30 people, 40 people, your family, your friends, your neighbors, your classmates, your classroom, your coworkers. Wherever you are—that is your platform, your stage, your circle of influence. That is your talk show, and that is where your power lies.

—*The Oprah Winfrey Show*, May 25, 2011

EVERYBODY WHO WORKS here at Harpo considers it a gift to have been able to serve all of you, our viewers. I have said many times that I have the best team in TV, and it's not just because they're great at what they do, not just because they work 17-hour days . . . it's because we all here are aligned with the vision of service to you, our viewers.

—*The Oprah Winfrey Show*, May 25, 2011

SAYING FAREWELL [to Harpo Studios and *The Oprah Winfrey Show*] was sobering, emotional and hard. It was also necessary. We had the greatest run in television history, but it was time to be realistic about going forward. About *growing* forward.

—*O, The Oprah Magazine*, May 2015

ON MY OWN I will just create, and if it works, it works, and if it doesn't, I'll create something else. I don't have any limitations on what I think I could do or be.

—*Forbes*, October 1995

Exploring

New Avenues

I ASKED MYSELF, I actually wrote it down, "What would I do if I wasn't afraid?" And I thought of what all the answers would be. Of course you would have a network. Of course you would build that platform and you would build it digitally and you would speak to the world and you would try to open people's hearts and you would let them see the best of themselves. That's what I would do if I wasn't afraid. . . . So I said, "Pretend you're not afraid and then take that step," and that is what I did.

— **interview with former Facebook COO**
Sheryl Sandberg, October 2, 2011

[*SNL* PRODUCER LORNE Michaels told me that] this thing that you've taken on is huge. It's big. And nobody wants to see you sashay from the set of *The Oprah Winfrey Show* into this new business and [have] everything go okay. You're going to have to pay your dues, you're going to have to learn the hard way.

—*Oprah Builds a Network*, **July 8, 2012**

LORNE MICHAELS [SAID] the channel will turn around when you get there, when you are physically present, and you are able to every day allow the words that you say and the vision that you hold to be executed in the way that you see fit. That's when it's going to change. You're going to have to physically put yourself there and you're going to have to physically take control.

—*Oprah Builds a Network*, July 8, 2012

I'M NOW UNDERSTANDING that your energy, your essence, your juice cannot be instilled unless you're actually there. You have to be in it first, then you have to empower everybody else to at least know what the vision is in such a way that they can execute it.

—*Oprah Builds a Network*, July 8, 2012

I ALSO UNDERSTAND that because I had a 25-year reputation that I built, that there was a big expectation [for OWN]. . . . And when we started with this network, I was the only person saying, "Let's not make it big, let's just start small, let's not do a big, big, big, big thing." Because you set an expectation that you cannot live up to. It's better for people to have lower expectations for you to overdeliver [on] rather than to underdeliver.

—*CBS This Morning*, April 2, 2012

I THINK THE expectation—and part of my own expectation—was I had 25 years of success, and I thought people would just leverage that into the network. Well, we didn't account for people not having the channel, not knowing how to find the channel, the cable audience being different than the broadcast audience, and more competition.

—*Hollywood Reporter*, December 19, 2012

[*THE OPRAH WINFREY Show*] was built around me and five producers. I'd go out and get the lunch for us—Taco Bell or Burger King. I prided myself on leanness. The opposite was done here [with OWN].

—*Wall Street Journal*, May 6, 2012

I KNEW THAT the three of us [Oprah along with OWN co-presidents Sheri Salata and Erik Logan] would have to join forces to lead our team to success. Even if that meant that we would have to go out into the field and be "boots to the ground" as new series started shooting. Whatever it took, we would have to do it.

—*Oprah Builds a Network*, July 8, 2012

I THINK OF every employee as a person first, as a human being with a family. We had many conversations about where we were as a company and how we were going to be able to sustain ourselves. And I knew from the time I stepped in as CEO [in July 2011] and started to sit in those meetings and look at the real numbers on the page, that the only way through is you're either going to have to end it, or you're going to have to make some cutbacks now so you'll be able to go forward. So the idea of having to let 30 people go, that was really rough. That was a tough decision.

—*Oprah Builds a Network*, July 15, 2012

MY HEART OVERFLOWS with gratitude to the people who stuck by me when the critics had called it quits for me and my "struggling" network. I grew to disdain the word struggle every time I saw it written to describe our state of affairs. But then I started to replace the narrative with gratitude. "I'm so grateful to have this opportunity to speak to the world in this way." . . . "I'm so grateful to be able to speak with a voice that's relevant to the issues of our times." When I shifted the paradigm to giving thanks, the work itself shifted.

—*O, The Oprah Magazine*, December 2013

I BELIEVE PEOPLE want to see television that is fun, that is entertaining, but that is also meaningful. What I want to do is use it as a platform for transforming people's lives . . . but if I see that that's not what the audience wants, then I will move on to the next thing.

—*CBS This Morning*, April 2, 2012

WE'RE BUILDING OUT one show at a time, 'til we get to 600 and then we'll get to 700 and eventually, 8,000.

—interview with former Facebook COO
Sheryl Sandberg, October 2, 2011
[on developing content for OWN]

I ONLY WANT the people with me who want to be with me. I only want the people who are in, who buy into the bigger, global mission and vision of what it is we're trying to do. We're not just creating a television network; we weren't just creating shows. And so I have said that is in the culture. You're here because you want to be a part of this big thing, this big and bigger thing that we are doing.

—interview with former Facebook COO
Sheryl Sandberg, October 2, 2011

I TRY TO surround myself with people who really know what they're doing and [then] give them the freedom to do it.

—*Fast Company*, October 12, 2015

I KNOW WHAT it's like to be part of a phenomenon. You can't create a phenomenon. You can't make it. You can't make it happen no matter how many publicity shots you do or how many times you try to get yourself in the press— you cannot create a phenomenon. The people do. It's the people's resonance and response to what it is you're putting out that creates the phenomenon.

—*Oprah Builds a Network*, July 15, 2012

I'VE TRIED TO surround myself with people who are all in, fully 100 percent for the next level of this mission, and who understand that it's not about creating more television shows. It's about connecting and speaking to the world in such a way that people . . . can begin to see the best of themselves. So we become a mirror to show them the best of themselves. And that is by carefully . . . selecting and gathering the tribe [of] people who want to be a part of that mission.

—interview with former Facebook COO
Sheryl Sandberg, October 2, 2011

I DON'T THINK the world needs another television channel. What the world needs is a different way of looking at itself. What the world needs is inspiration and light and exhilaration and stimulation and a little joy. What we need is to be able to look at the best of ourselves . . . instead of the lowest common denominator that so many television shows program to.

—interview with former Facebook COO
Sheryl Sandberg, October 2, 2011

WE NOW NEED 8,000 hours to fill a network. So I have to build the team. I'm in the process of taking the team that worked with me for 25 years on the *Oprah* show and combining that team with the team at OWN in Los Angeles to create a force so that it's not just me looking at all the shows and me making every decision. . . . I am one person and cannot do all of that.

—interview with former Facebook COO
Sheryl Sandberg, October 2, 2011

EVERYBODY WHO IS going to lead anything in their life—whether you're running your house, whether you're running multiple businesses—for a lot of that work, it's a guessing game. And it's really a guessing game until you can figure out, as we are still trying to do [with OWN], what is going to best serve [your] audience.

—*Oprah Builds a Network*, July 8, 2012

[I] REALLY, REALLY, really try to avoid meetings.

—*Fast Company*, October 12, 2015

WHEN I'M GOING to do an interview of significance, I always like to meet with the person before and ask them what do they really want, what is their intention, what do you want. Because I don't want to end the interview and you say, "Oh, you should have asked me" or "I thought you were going to ask me."

—*CBS Mornings*, **November 12, 2021**

I DON'T DO an interview if someone tells me I can't ask a certain question. My policy is, I can ask any question, you can tell me you won't answer it, but you have to tell me that on camera.

—*Hollywood Reporter*, **December 19, 2012**

I CERTAINLY NEVER planned to be on every cover, but trying to find a different celebrity each month was not a game any of us was up for.

—*O, The Oprah Magazine*, **December 2020 [on being pictured on the cover of *O, The Oprah Magazine*]**

WE ALL HOPE that when we write stories
that they will affect people. . . . But when you
actually see something tangible come from your
work, there's just no way to describe how good
that feels.

—*USA Today*, April 29, 2022

WHAT I LEARNED from all those conversations
that I had for all those years is that everybody
thinks they're right, and it's not my job to
prove them right or wrong but to give them the
opportunity to voice [their opinions], and we can
have a constructive conversation.

—*Wall Street Journal Magazine*, February 12, 2018

I WOULD ASK [my producers on the show] that
my voice, the words that I [choose], come from a
place that is centered, and centered in the desire
to be a force for good and connect in a way that
would be meaningful to people.

—interview with former LinkedIn CEO Jeff Weiner,
October 15, 2015

I CRAVE SILENCE. It's how I balance out the volume that's necessary to run a network and a magazine and remain somewhat sociable. What makes me *me* is being able to return to stillness.

—*O, The Oprah Magazine*, October 2014

KEEPING IT ALL straight is stressful. You need to give yourself moments to rest. I once told my assistant that just because I have ten free minutes on my calendar doesn't mean I want to fill them.

—*What I Know For Sure*, 2014

I USED TO do for every employee—now I have 700, so I can't—but I used to do what I call "the gut check." I would just spend a few minutes doing my own emotional check of how I felt about this person, whether I sensed their honesty.

—*Hollywood Reporter*, November 25, 2007

FOR 25 YEARS I had a schedule and a contract. Now the best thing ever is letting your body wake up when it wants to.

—*Wall Street Journal Magazine*, **February 12, 2018**

I WANT TO surround myself with people who are smarter than I am about what they do, particularly if it comes to technology and computers, because I can't get the damn TV on! I want them to do their jobs. And I want to give them the freedom and the allowance to do it as well as possible.

—*Entertainment Weekly*, **May 6, 2011**

I'd just like to be in the space where I really feel like I have nothing to prove.

—*Hollywood Reporter*, December 11, 2013

ARE YOU KIDDING? If you can't laugh at
yourself. . . . This is what people need to get about
this whole brand thing: My heart is my brand. . . .
Wherever I am, and [wherever] my heart is,
therein lies my brand. My heart is never going
to be tarnished. My heart is never going to be
ruined. My heart is never going to be taken down.

—*Oprah Builds a Network*, July 8, 2012 [on whether
her decision to spoof her brand and network on
Jimmy Kimmel Live! was risky]

ONE OF MY true roles on Earth is to be an
inspiration and to help people to connect to ideas
that inspire and expand their vision of who they
can be in the world. . . . My role is to break down
big ideas about who we are in a way that people
can see it and taste it and feel it and know it
for themselves.

—interview with former LinkedIn CEO Jeff Weiner,
October 15, 2015

NOTHING MAKES ME happier in my work—still to this day, if there's something in our magazine and someone writes and says, "You know, I read this article and I never thought of it this way before." [Those are] my favorite words.

—*Forbes* 400 Summit on Philanthropy, June 26, 2012

I DON'T CARE about being bigger, because I'm already bigger than I ever expected to be. My constant focus is on being better. Should I be doing multimedia video production? Or seminars on the Internet? How can I do what I'm already doing in a more forceful way?

—*Fortune*, April 1, 2002

On Leadership and Work Ethic

THE *BUCK* ALWAYS stops with me.

—**Oprah Winfrey Leadership Academy for Girls,
November 5, 2007**

IF I CAN'T take a risk, nobody can. What I have decided is that with fame, notoriety, credibility, if you can't have the courage then to stand up and speak out for what you truly believe in, then it means nothing.

—*Vogue*, **October 1998**

YOU NEVER WANT to be in a position where something is that important to you to do, and you can't do it because the boss says you can't. You want to be able to own yourself and make your own decisions about what's important to you to do.... So the fact that I had not been allowed the time [to film] *The Color Purple* is the reason why I made the decision to take the risk to own my own show. And that has made all the difference in the trajectory of my career.

—**speech at Stanford University, April 20, 2015**

WHEN I FIRST started being a "businesswoman,"
I worried about, "How do you do this?" And I
realized that you do this the same way as you do
anything else. You be fair. You try to be honest
with other people, and be fair.

—**Academy of Achievement, February 21, 1991**

I DIDN'T HAVE a lot of mentors, you know?
I happened into being a businesswoman. It
has never been a goal of mine, and I wouldn't
necessarily even say it's a strength of mine. . . .
I have to really work at it. I have to work at
disciplining myself. The business of the business
tires me out.

—*Hollywood Reporter*, **November 25, 2007**

I THINK THE higher up you go in the chain of capitalism, you experience it—sexism—huge. Because the expectation for who you are and what you should be doing as a woman—and as a Black woman—you know, you're breaking new ground and so people don't expect you to be sitting at certain board tables. People don't expect you to be able to break down certain barriers. They don't expect you. You sense it and you know it.

—*Larry King NOW*, January 4, 2018

I NEVER DID consider or call myself a feminist, but I don't think you can really be a woman in this world and not be.

—*Makers: Women Who Make America*,
February 26, 2013

[THE FAILURE OF the Oxygen network] was a great lesson for me: Don't partner when you're not allowed to be in charge and make a decision.

—*New York Times*, December 18, 2010

THE BIGGEST MISTAKE in the beginning was not understanding that you need infrastructure and systems in order to run a business. And that there's a reason why there's a hierarchy in reporting systems in business. You can't handle a business like friendship.

—*Hollywood Reporter*, **November 25, 2007**

ONE OF THE other big lessons that I've learned, particularly in business, is that you have a responsibility to yourself to learn as much about your business as you can.

—**Academy of Achievement, February 21, 1991**

PEOPLE REFER TO me as a brand now, the "Oprah Brand." I never knew what a brand was when I first started out—I didn't even know what that [meant]. I became a brand by making every decision flow from the truth of myself. Every choice I made, for every show that was going to be on the air, I made based on, "Does this feel right? ... Is this going to help somebody?"

—*Forbes* 400 Summit on Philanthropy, June 26, 2012

I ALWAYS PERSONALIZE [things] because that is my brand. For me, everything is personal.

—*Forbes* 400 Summit on Philanthropy, June 26, 2012

ONE OF THE lessons I learned from my school is that the same person it takes to build a school isn't the same person to carry on the school.

—*Hollywood Reporter*, May 26, 2011

I STAY IN my lane; I know what my lane is.

—interview at Stanford Graduate School of Business,
April 16, 2014

[MULTITASKING IS] A joke for me. When I try to
do that, I don't do anything well.

—*Fast Company*, October 12, 2015

THE WAY YOU step up your game is not to worry
about the other guy in any situation, because you
can't control the other guy. You only have control
over yourself. So it's like running a race. The
energy that it takes to look back and see where
the other guys are takes energy away from you. . . .
Don't waste your time in the race looking back to
see where the other guy is or what the other guy
is doing. It's not about the other guy. It's about
what can you do.

—Oprah's Master Class, March 27, 2011

I LEARNED TO do all my work as an offering that either could be received or not be received. And you do the work and then you let go of any attachment to how it's going to be received, or what people are going to say or whether or not they're going to like it. You just do the work with the intention.

—*Los Angeles Times*, April 29, 2022

A 12-HOUR DAY is a short day for me. I feel like, after a 12-hour day, "What am I going to do with the rest of my day?" I get home, and I don't know what to do with myself because I have all of this time left over. I don't know what to do. So I really feel most comfortable working 14 to 16 hours because then, at least, I can go home.

—**Academy of Achievement, February 21, 1991**

I AM REALLY good at working. Committed.
Diligent. With stamina on steroids. Playing, I'm
not so good at. I rarely decide to do anything
just for fun. So the question I've recently started
asking myself is, *Am I having a good time?* Am
I doing what I really want? What does fun
look like?

—*O, The Oprah Magazine*, **February 2015**

ONCE MY LIFE was mine to design, I found
myself a bit unbalanced in structuring it. I've
had to learn to plan what I want to do instead of
always fulfilling the "have to dos."

—*O, The Oprah Magazine*, **April 2015**

IF I LOST control of the business I'd lose
myself—or at least the ability to be myself.
Owning myself is a way to be myself.

—*Fortune*, **April 1, 2002**

ALL SUCCESS COMES with patience, and with patience comes power.

—*Hollywood Reporter*, December 19, 2012

YOU CAN'T KNOW who you are when you spend too much time on the mountaintop. You have to be taken down from the mountain in order to rise to the next level. There's no way you can accomplish anything of any value without having a challenge. Nobody just rides into anything. Nobody.

—*Oprah Builds a Network*, July 15, 2012

YOU CAN HAVE vision but unless you maintain leadership of the vision and are there to help oversee the execution of the vision, it doesn't work.

—*Hollywood Reporter*, December 19, 2012

THIS IS WHAT leadership is all about. To use your voice, no matter what the personal consequences, so that abuse will end and good will prevail.

—**Oprah Winfrey Leadership Academy for Girls,**
November 5, 2007

START WITH CLARITY of intention. Know yours and your opponent's. Make every deal a win-win. Otherwise, you lose long term.

—*Hollywood Reporter*, **December 10, 2015**

THE REAL KEY is not making emotional decisions ... [it's] starting with the infrastructure and the leadership that can sustain [projects] long term. . . . You have to have people whose vision is not only aligned with yours, but they also carry the passion for the vision as you do. . . . You need people who are equally as passionate about it as you are, and when you can do that, then you at least have a chance.

—*Forbes* **400 Summit on Philanthropy, June 26, 2012**

I KNOW THAT one of the things that is so important . . . is that you have leaders who are self-actualized and understand what your contribution to change the world can be. You can only do that if you know yourself. You cannot do that unless you take the time to actually know who you are and why you are here.

—interview at Stanford Graduate School of Business, April 16, 2014

I LOVE GIVING people opportunities where there might not have been one. Because somebody did that for me.

—*Variety*, October 6, 2015

PLAYING SMALL DOESN'T serve me. The truth is, I want millions of people. I'm not one of those people who says, "Oh, if I change just one person's life . . ." Nope, not satisfied with just a few. I want millions of people!

—*Fortune*, September 30, 2010

On Success and Wealth

I'M HERE TO tell you that your life isn't some big break, like everybody thinks it is.... It's actually about taking one significant, life-transforming step at a time.

—**commencement speech at Colorado College,
May 19, 2019**

I HAVE ALWAYS thought a mountain is a magnificent metaphor for life. From a distance, the ascent looks clear and smooth, but once you actually set out for the summit, you discover unexpected valleys and precarious ridges along the way. If your internal compass isn't set to keep climbing, every stumble will give you an excuse to turn back.

—*The Path Made Clear: Discovering Your
Life's Direction and Purpose*, 2019

IT'S VERY DIFFICULT for me to give myself
that credit. It's very difficult for me to even see
myself as successful because I still see myself
as in the process of becoming successful. To me,
"successful" is getting to the point where you are
absolutely comfortable with yourself. And it does
not matter how many things you have acquired.

—**Academy of Achievement, February 21, 1991**

I REALIZE THAT there is just a natural order to
things. When you're rising, people are pulling for
you as you rise. Once you reach a certain level,
if you go beyond what a person feels you should
be, then the opposite happens. Maya Angelou
said to me, "Be wary of those people who bow
at your feet, because when the winds of change
come, those same people will be at your throat."
I have always kept my distance from the acclaim
and the naysayers. I have maintained a sense of
center. I never got lost in it.

—*Chicago Tribune*, **May 20, 2011**

I TAKE CRITICISM very seriously. I can't say that I'm one of those people who does not read criticism because I do. And if someone criticizes something, and it strikes a nerve with me, I will then move to correct it. I have written to critics who said things that I thought were very valid.

—**Academy of Achievement, February 21, 1991**

OPPORTUNITIES, RELATIONSHIPS, EVEN money flowed my way when I learned to be grateful no matter what happened in my life.

—*O, The Oprah Magazine*, **November 2000**

THE KEY IS not to worry about being successful but to instead work toward being significant— and the success will naturally follow. How can you serve your way to greatness?

—*O, The Oprah Magazine*, **September 2001**

I BELIEVE IN service, I believe in helping people, I want people to feel fulfilled and empowered in their life, but still some days I think, "It's just cool to be me."

—interview with Michelle Obama, June 14, 2016

I'VE LEARNED THAT sometimes you have to step out of your ego to recognize the truth. So when life gets difficult, I've found that the best thing to do is ask myself a simple question: *What is this here to teach me?*

—*What I Know For Sure*, 2014

THE ABILITY TO learn to say "no" and not feel guilty about it is the greatest success I have achieved. For me to have the kind of internal strength and internal courage it takes to say, "No, I will not let you treat me this way," is what success is all about.

—Academy of Achievement, February 21, 1991

I LIVE BY the third law of motion in physics, which is for every action there is an equal and opposite reaction.... I know that what I'm thinking, and therefore [what I am] going to act on, is going to come back to me in a circular motion, just like gravity, like what goes up comes down. And so what also propels the action is the intention. So I don't do anything without being fully clear about why I intend to do it. Because the intention is going to determine the reaction, the result, or the consequence in every circumstance.

—interview at Stanford Graduate School of Business,
April 16, 2014

EVERY TIME WE have seen a person on this stage who [has] success in their life, they spoke of the joy and they spoke of the juice that they receive from doing what they knew they were meant to be doing.

—*The Oprah Winfrey Show*, May 25, 2011

THERE'S NO QUESTION that changing the way you think about your situation is the key to improving it. I know for sure that all of our hurdles have meaning. And being open to learning from those challenges is the difference between succeeding and getting stuck.

—What I Know For Sure, 2014

YOU CANNOT FULFILL [your greater purpose] unless you have a level of self-awareness. [You need] to be connected to what is the inner voice or instinct—I call it the "emotional GPS system"—that allows you to make the best decisions for yourself. And every decision that has profited me has come from me listening to that inner voice first. Every time I have gotten into a situation where I was in trouble, it's because I didn't listen to it.

—interview at Stanford Graduate School of Business, April 16, 2014

IT DOESN'T MATTER how far you might rise. At some point, you are bound to stumble because ... if you are constantly pushing yourself higher [and] higher, the law of averages, not to mention the myth of Icarus, predicts that you will at some point fall. And when you do, I want you to know this, remember this: There is no such thing as failure. Failure is just life trying to move us in another direction.

—**commencement speech at Harvard University, May 30, 2013**

ONE OF MY greatest lessons has been to fully understand that what looks like a dark patch in the quest for success is the universe pointing you in a new direction.

—***What I Know For Sure*, 2014**

THE ONLY REASON to be a person whom everybody knows, who is successful, is to transmit the message of successfulness, to say, "That is possible."

—*Makers: Women Who Make America,*
February 26, 2013

I THINK PART of the reason I am as successful as I have been is because the success wasn't the goal—the process was. I wanted to do good work. I wanted to do well in my life.

—*60 Minutes*, **December 14, 1986**

IT'S IMPORTANT TO me to remain consistent in my ideas and consistent in whatever it is I'm trying to offer.

—*The goop Podcast*, **March 7, 2018**

I DON'T KNOW if anybody really skyrockets to success. I think that success is a process. And I believe that my first Easter speech, at Kosciusko Baptist Church, at the age of three and a half, was the beginning. And that every other speech, every other book I read, every other time I spoke in public, was a building block. So that by the time I first sat down to audition in front of a television camera, and somebody said, "Read this," what allowed me to read it so comfortably and be so at ease with myself at that time, was the fact that I had been doing it a while. If I'd never read a book, or never spoken in public before, I would have been traumatized by it.

—**Academy of Achievement, February 21, 1991**

I'VE BEEN VERY poor in my life, and so the idea of having money and not being responsible and knowing how much money you have and keeping control of it, is not something that I personally can accept.

—**Academy of Achievement, February 21, 1991**

I STILL SAVE toast. I do. I will save a toast rather than throw it away. And I know there's going to be more toast, but I still do because there's something in me because when we were growing up, we had to save it. You know, you weren't allowed to, like, throw food away.

—"Oprah's 2020 Vision: Your Life in Focus" tour, January 25, 2020

WHEN YOU'RE THE most successful person in your family, in your neighborhood and in your town, everybody thinks you're the First National Bank and you have to figure out for yourself where those boundaries are.

—*Hollywood Reporter*, December 11, 2013

ULTIMATELY, YOU HAVE to make money because you are a business. I let other people worry about that. I worry about the message. I am always, always, always about holding true to the vision and the message, and when you are true to that, then people respond.

—*New York Times*, November 25, 2012

ALL THESE YEARS later, I am still keenly aware that I am not my salary. I give thanks every day for having the opportunity not only to make a living but to create what I see as an exquisite life. And I know that everyone needs a source of income in order to survive. But I have come to believe that one of the reasons I've enjoyed financial success is because my focus has never been on money.

—*The Path Made Clear: Discovering Your Life's Direction and Purpose,* 2019

WHAT I KNOW for sure is that no matter how much wealth you come to possess, everything passes and changes with time. What is real, what is forever, is who you are and what you are meant to share with the world.

—*The Path Made Clear: Discovering Your Life's Direction and Purpose,* 2019

AND I MAKE no apologies for it. Because
I worked to earn it. Nobody gave it to me,
I didn't have a father that took over the
business or a husband who left me money,
or uncles who helped me. I feel completely
responsible for having created the life that I
have and also equally grateful and blessed for
it. But I understand that it is a very blessed and
privileged life that gives you access to healthcare,
access to whatever you need, in a way that many
people do not.

—*Los Angeles Times*, **April 29, 2022**

THE IDEA OF being able to have anything you
want and buy anything you want and not to have
that as a worry . . . it's all relative. I mean, how
much money can you spend in a lifetime? And
after you have the house you want, or the houses
you want, or the car or cars or shoes or whatever,
the square footage, you want, then what? So it
puts you in a space . . . to think about the broader
picture of really, why am I here?

—*Larry King NOW*, **January 4, 2018**

I BELIEVE IN real estate. I love property the way some women love shoes.

> —"Oprah's 2020 Vision: Your Life in Focus" tour, January 25, 2020

OH, YOU RENTING [a home] and buying a Rolex? You should definitely own if you're buying a Rolex.

> —"Oprah's 2020 Vision: Your Life in Focus" tour, January 25, 2020

A LOT OF people wish they had my money. It's jealousy and self-hatred.... You aren't saying I shouldn't have it, are you?

> —*New York Times,* June 11, 1989

The Importance of Helping Others

PICK A PROBLEM—ANY problem—and do something about it. Because to somebody who's hurting, something is everything.

> —commencement speech at University of Southern California's Annenberg School for Communication and Journalism, May 11, 2018

WE'RE ALL CONFUSED about fame versus service in this country.

> —*The Oprah Winfrey Show*, May 25, 2011

THAT QUESTION OF "How do we serve the viewer?" transformed [*The Oprah Winfrey Show*]. And because we asked that question every single day from 1989 forward—with the intention of only doing what was in service to the people who were watching—it is why, no matter where I go in the world, on any given day somebody comes up to me and says, "I watched your show, it changed my life." . . . That happened because of an intention to be of service.

> —commencement speech at Colorado College, May 19, 2019

THE KEY TO realizing a dream is to focus not on success but on service. Ask yourself, what are the gifts and talents you can share to raise the collective consciousness of all that you encounter?

—*The Wisdom of Sundays*, 2017

I THINK PHILANTHROPY should come out of you: Your doing should come out of your being.

**—interview at Stanford Graduate School of Business,
April 16, 2014**

[IT'S ABOUT] UNDERSTANDING the greater vision, purpose, and calling of whatever your philanthropic efforts are [and] holding on to what you really intended—what is the larger vision for what you're trying to do? It's what Stephen Covey has often called "beginning with the end in mind." Holding the end in mind is what has gotten me through every crisis, either [in] business or philanthropically.

—*Forbes* 400 Summit on Philanthropy, June 26, 2012

THE REAL REWARD comes when you have true engagement in what it is that you choose to give.

—*Forbes* **400 Summit on Philanthropy, June 26, 2012**

TRUE PHILANTHROPY COMES from living from the heart of yourself and giving what you have been given. How will you do that? How will you use your personality, the energy of your personality, to serve that which is your soul's calling? I know this for sure: any life—no matter how fantastic it is, how glorious it seems, how much attention you receive, how much square footage you have—any life and every life is enhanced by the sharing and the giving and the opening up of the heart space. Your life gets better when you can find a way to share it with someone else.

—**speech at *Variety*'s Power of Women luncheon, October 9, 2015**

IT IS A beautiful thing to receive an award. It's a beautiful thing, but the true reward is in the lives that you are able to touch and the people who you know you have impacted.

—speech at *Variety*'s Power of Women luncheon, October 9, 2015

WHEN YOU INVEST in a girl, you change a community.... In every study that's ever been done, if a woman is educated, if a girl is educated, she's going to educate her children. If a girl is educated ... she's more likely to have fewer children. She's more likely to use protection, to take care of herself and her children. She's more likely to then take what she knows and share that with her entire community.

—interview with former Facebook COO Sheryl Sandberg, October 2, 2011

EVERYBODY WANTS A leader, a savior, a solution. But there isn't one. It's not one thing—it's every thing. Everyday acts of goodwill and consciousness are what's needed to restore our collective broken soul.

—*O, The Oprah Magazine*, **January 2019**

EVERY ACTION YOU take has consequences you can't foresee. It's the ripple effect. And when your actions are done with the intention of helping others, the ripples are wonderful to behold.

—*O, The Oprah Magazine*, **March 2020**

Use your life to serve the world and you will discover the myriad ways the world offers itself to serve you.

—*The Wisdom of Sundays*, 2017

WHAT THIS [COVID-19] pandemic has done is made me think about giving differently. How I give and who's on the receiving end of that, and how do you do that in such a way that sustains people? I've ultimately always believed that you teach people to fish ... but sometimes people just need fish and a piece of bread. Sometimes you need some fish, OK? Sometimes you don't have time to learn to fish.

—**Associated Press, May 20, 2020**

ISN'T IT AMAZING how ... you start out wanting to offer your services, you know, lift somebody up, and you end up getting lifted yourself? That the reward is far more than you ever imagined?

—***Oprah's Super Soul**, June 3, 2018*

DEVELOP A NEW vision of service to others, to your family, community, and world. Lift yourself out of the mundane to magnificent heights. If you honor your calling, your life will be blessed.

—convocation address at the Kellogg School of Management, June 16, 2001

THE WAY TO be of service is to answer the call for yourself—what is it you want to do and you want to give?—not to be confused by the voices of the world telling you what you're supposed to do.

—interview with former Facebook COO Sheryl Sandberg, October 2, 2011

WE'RE ALL TRYING to be here on the planet and fulfill what it is our heart wants to express. When you can figure out a thing that connects with you, there really isn't anything better. I feel expanded because of the work that I do that's called charity.

—*Variety*, October 6, 2015

WHAT OTHER PEOPLE view as successful is not what my idea of success is. And I don't mean to belittle it at all. It's really nice to be able to have nice things. What material success does is provide you with the ability to concentrate on other things that really matter. And that is being able to make a difference, not only in your own life, but in other people's lives.

—**Academy of Achievement, February 21, 1991**

YOU FIRST HAVE to change the way a person thinks and sees themselves. So you've gotta create a sense of aspiration, a sense of hopefulness, so a person can see, can begin to even have a vision for a better life.

—**interview at Stanford Graduate School of Business, April 16, 2014**

YOU CAN BE the kind of person who writes the biggest check and think nothing else about it, and you do it because that's good for your portfolio or it's good for a tax write-off, or you can be the kind of person who doesn't have a lot to give, but reaches inside to the truth in the core of yourself, and you give that. And that person is rewarded exponentially.

—*Forbes* **400 Summit on Philanthropy, June 26, 2012**

SOME DAYS THE awareness of the sanctity and sacredness of life brings me to my knees with gratitude. I'm still trying to wrap my head around the idea that the little girl from Mississippi who grew up holding her nose in an outhouse now flies on her own plane—my own plane!—to Africa to help girls who grew up like her.

—*What I Know For Sure,* **2014**

Part 3

LIFE LESSONS

Race and Politics

MISSISSIPPI IN THE time I was born was the most racist state in the United States. You wouldn't want to be caught after dark if you were a Black person in Mississippi. They had absolutely no regard for your humanity—they didn't even think you were human. The fact that I could be born at that time and now do what I do, am who I am, live where I live is the most extraordinary story I can ever imagine.

—*Oprah's Master Class: The Podcast*, **January 30, 2019**

I'M 10 YEARS old at my mom's place in Milwaukee. It's 1964 and Black people are still "colored" and they're not riding in limousines unless their kinfolk have just died. I press my knees into the cold linoleum and stare into our black-and-white TV. My mouth falls open when Sidney Poitier wins the Academy Award for Best Actor. I cried tears of joy for him and for the hope and possibility that moment represented. It changed who I thought I could be.

—**Facebook, August 16, 2022**

I AM A student of the civil rights movement. I understand very clearly that I get to sit in the seat that I hold in life because there are a lot of people who paved the way for me.

—*Live with Kelly and Michael*, December 19, 2014

I UNDERSTAND, BEING a student of the world, looking at not just racism in our country and oppression in other countries, wherever there is someone who is the superior, there's always— human nature—the feeling of "I've got to make myself feel like I've got to kick someone about." And so I understand that, and part of my role is to mitigate that.

—*Larry King NOW*, January 4, 2018

WE SEE, ALMOST on a regular daily basis, racism rearing its ugly head in ways that without body cams and cameras, a lot of people could not have imagined.

—*Oprah's Super Soul*, June 6, 2018

WHEN I THINK about the African American community, I see how trauma can trace back for generations—all the way back to slavery. Hundreds of years of internalizing the trauma of racism, segregation, brutality, fear, and the dismantling of the nuclear family—all of it replicated and repeated over and over at the micro level of the individual and eventually seen and felt at the macro level of society. That's why the Black Lives Matter protests of 2020 were so powerful. The individual at the micro level and society at the macro level had both reached an apex of pain.

—*What Happened to You?*, 2021

I WAS TRYING to explain it this way: I have a
fear of pit bulls. I love dogs. I have five dogs. I've
had 21 dogs in my lifetime, but I have a fear of
pit bulls. And it doesn't matter what you tell
me about pit bulls, I have this conscious and
unconscious belief that a pit bull will turn on me,
a pit bull will hurt me. That is my unconscious
belief, whether that is true or not. I think that
to many white people—many of them police
officers—Black men, Brown men are like
pit bulls.

—Oprah's Super Soul, June 6, 2018

I WAS ON trial in 1998 for saying something
bad about a burger. I was on trial for six weeks
in Texas, and I remember thinking every day,
what if the sentencing here was not just money
or a fine . . . but what if the sentencing was that I
would have to go to jail for something that I knew
I didn't do? I thought about, for the first time in a
real way, all the people who were in jail for things
they didn't do and how horrible that must be.

—Oprah's Super Soul, June 13, 2018

THE TRUTH EXONERATES and it convicts. It disinfects and it galvanizes. The truth has always been and will always be our shield against corruption, our shield against greed and despair. The truth is our saving grace.

—commencement speech at University of Southern California's Annenberg School for Communication and Journalism, May 11, 2018

THE PANDEMIC HAS illuminated the vast systemic inequities that have defined life for too many for too long. For poor communities without adequate access to healthcare, inequality is a preexisting condition. For immigrant communities forced to hide in the shadows, inequality is a preexisting condition. For incarcerated people with no ability to social-distance, inequality is a preexisting condition. For every person burdened by bias and bigotry, for every Black [person] living in their American skin, fearful to even go for a jog, inequality is a preexisting condition.

—virtual commencement speech for "#Graduation 2020: Facebook and Instagram Celebrate the Class of 2020" event, May 15, 2020

WHEN YOU HEAR yourself saying, "It doesn't matter what one person says," "Oh well, so what, it's not going to make any difference what I do, who cares?" When you hear yourself saying that, know that you are on a collision course for our culture. . . . These times are here to let us know that we need to take a stand for our right to have hope. We need to take a stand with every ounce of wit and courage we can muster.

—commencement speech at University of Southern California's Annenberg School for Communication and Journalism, May 11, 2018

BEYOND ALL THE policy issues that will matter most in the future—the economy, climate change, healthcare, Social Security, education—what's really at stake are civility, decency, *humanity*.

—*O, The Oprah Magazine*, November 2020

ONE OF THE great things about our democracy is that every citizen can decide to run for public office.

—*Washington Post*, December 31, 2021

I THINK THERE is so much negativity on both sides—red states and blue states—and people are rising to the level of hysteria to meet each one, that there are far more people leaning purple than ever before.

—*Oprah's Super Soul*, June 27, 2018

LISTEN, I'VE LOOKED in the eyes of murderers and child molesters and all kinds of people who have done terrible things. I can definitely listen to somebody who has a different political view.

—*Wall Street Journal Magazine*, February 12, 2018

IN THAT POLITICAL structure—all the non-truths, the bullshit, the crap, the nastiness, the backhanded backroom stuff that goes on—I feel like I could not exist. . . . It's not a clean business. It would kill me.

—*British Vogue*, August 2018 [on running for president]

I DON'T RECOGNIZE a country where you've lost nearly a million people [to the COVID-19 pandemic] and there hasn't been some form of remembering that is significant. Not at the opening of a speech or mentioning in a State of the Union. I mean that there hasn't been a communal gathering where there is acknowledgment that this has happened to us. Who are we that there is no acknowledgment, profoundly, in our society that we have lost our loved ones?

—*Los Angeles Times*, **April 29, 2022**

ONE PROFOUND THING I realized, after listening to thousands of people share their story, is that all pain is the same—we just choose different ways to express it. And beyond that, I believe we are all here to learn from one another's pain. So the loss of community and the social isolation we all feel is a source of great collective pain.

—*What Happened to You?*, **2021**

THIS IS THE problem as I see it in public discourse: People become hysterical because you try and meet their energy, but you have to be bigger than that. You have to try and transcend— you can't go toe-to-toe.

—*Wall Street Journal Magazine*, **February 12, 2018**

I LOVE THAT Juneteenth is now an official federal holiday. A time to honor our past and those who've forged a path to our present.

—**Facebook, June 19, 2021**

AS WE GATHERED in fellowship to honor our sister Judge Ketanji Brown Jackson's new appointment to the Supreme Court, something that took 232 years to achieve, we leaned into the deep-rooted triumph that our ancestors may not have even been able to dream of, let alone see come to fruition.

—**Facebook, April 12, 2022**

Achieving Balance

JUST BECAUSE YOU have all of these demands on your time and on you doesn't mean that you have to say yes. . . . Understanding that really changed the meaning of my life in that I was no longer driven by what other people wanted me to do.

—speech at Stanford University, April 20, 2015

WHETHER YOU HAVE a week to laze around or a 20-minute break between errands, I promise it's possible to truly relax.

—*O, The Oprah Magazine*, July 2015

I WORK HARD and play well; I believe in the yin and yang of life. It doesn't take a lot to make me happy because I find satisfaction in so much of what I do. Some satisfactions are higher-rated than others, of course. And because I try to practice what I preach—living in the moment—I am consciously attuned most of the time to how much pleasure I am receiving.

—*What I Know For Sure*, 2014

WHO COULDN'T USE a little refresh now and again? I'm a big fan of the kinds of minor changes that add up to major delight—a quick swap, a brilliant fix, a more efficient strategy—and I'm betting you are, too.

—O, The Oprah Magazine, September 2014

I REALLY DON'T define my happiness by my business decisions.

—Fortune, April 1, 2002

IT WILL ONLY get worse if you don't learn to manage your time now. And it's yours to design.

—O, The Oprah Magazine, June 2015

WE ALL GET the opportunity to feel wonder every day, but we've been lulled into numbness. Have you ever driven home from work, opened your front door, and asked yourself how you got there? I know for sure that I don't want to live a shut-down life—desensitized to feeling and seeing. I want every day to be a fresh start on expanding what is possible.

—*What I Know For Sure*, 2014

STAYING PRESENT IS the reason, after talking to thousands of people over the years, I still have aha moments. Meaningful things happen when you release the anxious thoughts and negative chatter that's in your head and tune in to what the person in front of you is saying.

—*The Wisdom of Sundays*, 2017

I LIVE IN the moment. People are saying to me, how are you going to top this? It's not my desire to top it, my desire is to keep manifesting for myself the life I was meant to live, and so that could take me anywhere.

—People, **May 30, 2005**

YOUR PRIMARY JOB is to take care of yourself. You've got to decide to make your health and well-being your priority; otherwise you run out of oxygen.

—O, The Oprah Magazine, **June 2015**

EVER NOTICE HOW often you unconsciously hold your breath? Once you start paying attention, it might surprise you to see how much tension you've been carrying around inside. Nothing is more effective than a deep, slow inhale and release for surrendering what you can't control and focusing again on what's right in front of you.

—What I Know For Sure, **2014**

I'M NOT NEARLY as stressed as people might imagine. Over the years, I've learned to focus my energy on the present, to be fully aware of what's happening in every moment and not to worry about what should have happened, what's going wrong, or what might come next.

—*What I Know For Sure*, 2014

THE NUMBER ONE principle that rules my life is intention.

—interview with former LinkedIn CEO Jeff Weiner, October 15, 2015

BECOME THE CHANGE you want to see—those are words I live by. Instead of belittling, uplift. Instead of demolishing, rebuild. Instead of misleading, light the way so that all of us can stand on higher ground.

—*What I Know For Sure*, 2014

ALL OF US need a vision for our lives.... Success comes when you surrender to that dream—and let it lead you to the next best place.

—*O, The Oprah Magazine*, September 2001

HAVE THE COURAGE to follow your passion— and if you don't know what it is, realize that one reason for your existence on earth is to find it.

—*O, The Oprah Magazine*, September 2001

HOW DO YOU know whether you're on the right path, with the right person, or in the right job? The same way you know when you're not. You feel it.

—*O, The Oprah Magazine*, September 2001

THE GREATEST LESSON from that experience [making the film *Beloved*] is to do your best, enjoy the journey, and then release all attachment to what is to come. Let it be. And be comfortable with whatever it is.

—*O, The Oprah Magazine*, February 2001

YOU UNDERSTAND THAT when you know better, you ought to do better—and doing better sometimes means changing your mind; and you realize that letting go of what others think you should do is the only way to reach your full potential.

—*O, The Oprah Magazine*, June 2001

AS I OFTEN tell my girls [attending the Oprah Winfrey Leadership Academy for Girls] from atop my "Mom O" perch, a career is not a life. What you want to do should emerge from who you want to be. *Who do you want to be?* That, to me, is the essential question.

—*O, The Oprah Magazine*, April 2014

Spirituality

I START MY morning with some rousing gospel to wake up my mind, body, and soul. It takes me back to my childhood and also unites me with my ancestors.

—**Facebook, April 16, 2022**

WHO I AM is grounded specifically in my sense of spiritual worth and value—to myself, to the planet, to the universe, to God.

—*Oprah's Master Class: The Podcast*, **January 30, 2019**

I WOULD HAVE to say one of the fundamental turning points in my life was *The Color Purple*. Nothing has had a greater impact on me—spiritually, emotionally, psychologically—in determining my path, because it literally changed my faith, in that, I could see it. It was real. It was real. God can dream a bigger dream for me, for you, than you could ever dream for yourself.

—*Oprah's Master Class: The Podcast*, **February 6, 2019**

YOUR SOUL IS as unique as your fingerprint. And the journey to connect to the deepest part of yourself can only be explored by you.

—*The Wisdom of Sundays*, 2017

I AM A big soul. The way you know if you're a big soul: your soul's influence is in direct proportion to the amount of people you are able to affect. There are smaller souls that are equally as powerful in their fields. Just because you cannot reach a lot of people doesn't mean that you don't have the same impact on the amount of people that you are reaching.

—*The goop Podcast*, March 7, 2018

FAILURE, DISAPPOINTMENT, AND heartbreak can expand our souls if we're willing to face our truths.

—Facebook, June 11, 2017

WHEN YOU HONOR what you know your spirit is telling you to do, you are making the most conscientious decision, one for which you are willing to accept all the consequences.

—*O, The Oprah Magazine*, June 2001

WHAT I KNOW for sure is the most valuable gift you can give yourself is the time to nurture the unique spirit that is you.

—*The Wisdom of Sundays*, 2017

I BELIEVE EVERY one of us is born with a purpose. No matter who you are, what you do, or how far you think you have to go, you have been tapped by a force greater than yourself to step into your God-given calling. This goes far beyond what you do to earn your living. I'm talking about a supreme moment of destiny, the reason you are here on earth.

—*The Path Made Clear: Discovering Your Life's Direction and Purpose*, 2019

SPIRITUALITY FOR ME is recognizing that I am connected to the energy of all creation, that I am a part of it and it is always a part of me.

—*The Wisdom of Sundays*, 2017

ANYONE WHO'S ON the path of a spiritual awakening needs to know that it's sometimes difficult.... But I don't see the opportunity to craft our own lives as a burden. I see it as one of the gifts of being alive.

—*The Wisdom of Sundays*, 2017

ALL OF US have a limited number of years here on earth. What do you want to do with yours? How do you want to spend your precious, ever-unfolding future? There's no need to waste another day wondering if there's more to life. There is. And it's yours for the finding.

—*The Path Made Clear: Discovering Your Life's Direction and Purpose*, 2019

MY GOAL IS to live my life as a more awakened, vibrant, alive human being. My prayer is to not let any moment pass without my acknowledgment and full experience of it. In order to do that, I've got to practice.

—*The Wisdom of Sundays*, 2017

GRATITUDE IS ITS own energy field. When you acknowledge and are grateful for whatever you have, it allows more to be drawn to you and changes the way you experience life. Grace is transformative. The more grateful you are, the more grace mirrors the gratitude that you have.

—*The Wisdom of Sundays*, 2017

I DEFINE MYSELF as a universal human. I sense the threads of consciousness that connect us all. And I believe our collective *unconsciousness* regarding our earth and all her children—our neglect and ill treatment—could eventually be our undoing.

—*O, The Oprah Magazine*, April 2019

THE GREAT REWARD for me is knowing that what I'm doing and how I've done it and how I choose to live in the space that I call God—how in God I move and breathe and have my being and I try to move from the center of that—is able to literally touch the lives of other people.

—speech at *Variety*'s Power of Women luncheon, October 9, 2015

MY ROLE AND my goal in life is to open people's hearts. That's what I do, is I try to tell stories that allow people to see themselves in the lives of other people.

—*Larry King NOW*, January 4, 2018

I BELIEVE IN signs. They fill me with wonder. Because I know for sure: Each and every one of us is a part of the Life force. We don't *have* a life. We *are* Life, expressed in human form.

—*O, The Oprah Magazine*, December 2019

I am probably one of the most content, peaceful people you will ever meet.

—*Wall Street Journal Magazine*, February 12, 2018

I KNOW BY now that life speaks first in whispers. When we don't listen, the whispers get louder. Messages unheeded turn into problems and eventually crises.

—*O, The Oprah Magazine*, December 2019

WHEN THE UNIVERSE compels me toward the best path to take, it never leaves me with "Maybe," "Should I?" or even "Perhaps." I always know for sure when it's telling me to proceed— because everything inside me rises up to reverberate "Yes!"

—*What I Know For Sure*, 2014

I'VE REALIZED THAT despite all the time I've spent running and doing and doing, the quiet, sweet stillness of just being with myself is the greatest peace.

—*O, The Oprah Magazine*, July/August 2020

I ACTUALLY THINK death is going to be quite a surprise. You know that movie, *The Piano*, when Holly Hunter goes underneath [the water] and the piano drags her down and the first thing she says: "Ah, death. What a surprise?" I'm not looking forward to it, but you know, we're not going to get out of it.

—*Larry King NOW*, **January 4, 2018**

I OFTEN FEEL that when people—someone close to you passes, you now have an angel you can call by name. And in spirit, you can feel them in ways you couldn't in the flesh.

—**"Oprah's 2020 Vision: Your Life in Focus" tour, January 25, 2020**

Relationships

LIFE IS BETTER when you share it.

—*Forbes* **400 Summit on Philanthropy, June 26, 2012**

AS AN ADULT, I am grateful to enjoy long-term, consistent, loving relationships with many people. Yet the early beatings, emotional fractures, and splintered connections that I experienced with the central figures in my early life no doubt helped develop my solitary independence. In the powerful words of the poem "Invictus," *I am the master of my fate, I am the captain of my soul.*

—*What Happened to You?*, **2021**

RESPECT IS THE foundation of ALL relationships, no matter how young you are or how young the person you're interacting with is. Surround yourself with people who bring you their light and who you can give them your light.

—**Facebook, May 2, 2021**

EVERYBODY JUST WANTS to know that you hear me and that you see me.

> —"Oprah's 2020 Vision: Your Life in Focus" tour,
> February 8, 2020

ALL OF [OUR] arguments are really about the same thing: It's about, "Did you hear me? Did you see me? And did what I say mean anything to you?"

> —interview at Stanford Graduate School of Business,
> April 16, 2014

EVERYTHING I DO—MY work on TV, my engagement with my school [The Oprah Winfrey Leadership Academy for Girls], my interactions with business partners and personal friends— arises from who I choose to be. And daily, we each get to choose. . . . What kind of person do you want to be?

> —*O, The Oprah Magazine*, April 2014

[MAYA ANGELOU] WAS the mother figure to me. My biological mother didn't have the opportunity to be educated. Being raised in the South, being a domestic worker her whole life, she didn't have the opportunities that Maya Angelou, so fortunately, had been exposed to. My mother couldn't give me what Maya had. I needed a mother like Maya to mentor me through this whole fame process. She was my grounding tool for it all. I learned my greatest lessons from her. She was my comfort, she was my nurturer, she was my inspiration. She was the person who would say, "You can do it, babe, you can do it." She'd say, "Take it all the way." . . . Even now, when something goes very right and something goes very wrong, her spirit abides with mine. And I verbally call on her.

—*The goop Podcast*, **March 7, 2018**

SOMETIMES I THINK [Maya Angelou] didn't so much pass away from me as she passed into me.

—*Food, Health, and Happiness: 115 On-Point Recipes*
for Great Meals and a Better Life, **2017**

I really never seriously considered having children because I was not willing to make the sacrifice required, and I do see it as an ultimate sacrifice. I think that the decision to have a child is a decision that you make in sacrifice. And so, I didn't have children because I knew that to have the life that I have, and to be able to create the platform that I have, it was more important for me to be a teacher.

—*Oprah's Master Class: The Podcast*, February 6, 2019

The reason why I didn't have children and don't regret [not] having children is because the show became my life.

—interview with Barbara Walters, December 9, 2010

I never had therapy because I had the *Oprah* show, so I told all of my business out there on the streets, and also because I had Gayle [King] to talk to every night.

—"Oprah's 2020 Vision: Your Life in Focus" tour, January 25, 2020

I CAN TELL you in my entire life, I never call my mother or my father to tell them anything like I got a new job or I met a new guy or I got a car . . . none of that, so Gayle served as my chosen family and the person who stood in the gap for me.

—*People,* **April 26, 2022**

IT'S RARE THAT I make a big decision without asking Gayle King for her input. Of course, even if I didn't ask, Gayle would offer. That's the kind of person she is, and that's fine with me.

—*O, The Oprah Magazine,* **September 2019**

I REALIZED: "OH Gayle was what I used for my sense of regulation," and is still the person in my life. . . . I have probably three people in my life who are going to tell me the truth no matter what.

—*The Independent,* **April 26, 2022**

FOR YEARS PEOPLE have marveled at our friendship and sometimes misunderstood it. But anyone who has a soulful bond with a friend, a friend who would do anything for you, who revels in your happiness and is there to comfort you in your sadness, gets it exactly.

—*O, The Oprah Magazine*, September 2019
[on best friend Gayle King]

WHO KNEW A snowstorm 46 years ago would gift us a friendship of almost five decades?

—Facebook, April 27, 2022
[on being snowed in with Gayle King in 1976]

I WAS JUST some place the other day and somebody said, "This is my Gayle" . . . and I understand what that means.

—*People*, April 26, 2022

I believe three of the most important words anyone can say are not I love you, but I hear you.

—The Wisdom of Sundays, 2017

I UNDERSTAND WHY people think we're gay.
There isn't a definition in our culture for this
kind of bond between women. So I get why
people have to label it—how can you be this close
without it being sexual? How else can you explain
a level of intimacy where someone *always* loves
you, *always* respects you, admires you?

—*O, The Oprah Magazine*, August 2006

HE'S KIND AND supportive. Lots of people
want to ride with you in the limo. But you want
someone who'll help you catch the bus.

—*People*, November 23, 1992
[on long-term partner Stedman Graham]

I REALIZED I didn't actually want a marriage.
I wanted to be *asked*. I wanted to know he felt I
was worthy of being his missus, but I didn't want
the sacrifices, the compromises, the day-in-day-
out commitment required to make a marriage
work. My life with the show was my priority, and
we both knew it.

—*O, The Oprah Magazine*, February 2020

BOTH HE AND I now say, "If we had married, we would not be together." No question about it—we would not stay married, because of what that would have meant to him, and I would have had my own ideas about it.

—*People*, October 9, 2019

THAT IS SO good, when you can have a partner . . . a spiritual partnership, when you have a partnership between equals for the purpose of spiritual growth. Meaning you're growing together in spirit. You're there for one another.

—"Oprah's 2020 Vision: Your Life in Focus" tour, January 25, 2020

Advice for Living Your Best Life

DON'T LET PEOPLE talk you into what they think is you.

—*Hollywood Reporter*, December 11, 2013

I HAVE LEARNED that your full-on attention for any activity you choose to experience comes with a level of intensity and truth. It's about living a present life, moment to moment—not worrying about what's going to happen at 3 o'clock and what's going to happen at 7 o'clock.

—*Fast Company*, October 12, 2015

MY GREATEST ADVICE to you is to surround yourself with people who are going to fill your cup until your cup runneth over.

—commencement speech at Spelman College, May 20, 2012

No matter what triumphs, defeats, sad times, painful times, whatever you have to go through in life—you are your own best thing.

—*New York Times*, May 24, 2011

I'm keenly aware that every day is a gift, that time is fleeting. Another year has passed. So quickly gone. No moment but this one is guaranteed, so I'm ready to be in each as the healthiest, strongest, fittest, most conscious, most alive me I've ever been.

—*O, The Oprah Magazine*, January 2016

Let me ask you something: Have you ever posed a question to yourself that shifted your point of view? Maybe, *Is this what I really want?* or *What's my next move?* Over the years, I've asked myself many questions like these, from *What do I know for sure?* . . . to *What am I doing that's working?* . . . I've learned that big-picture pondering can have life-changing effects.

—*O, The Oprah Magazine*, April 2014

WHEN YOU DON'T know what to do, my best advice is to do nothing until clarity comes. Getting still, being able to hear your own voice and not the voices of the world, quickens clarity. Once you decide what you want, make a commitment to that decision.

—*What I Know For Sure*, 2014

WHEN YOU'RE DOWN in the hole, when that moment comes, it's really okay to feel bad for a little while. Give yourself time to mourn what you think you may have lost. But then—here's the key—learn from every mistake. Because every experience, encounter, and particularly your mistakes are there to teach you and force you into being more of who you are.

—commencement speech at Harvard University,
May 30, 2013

I BELIEVE THAT resilience is the single most important quality that allows human beings to triumph in moments of difficulty.

—Facebook, May 3, 2022

IF CHANGE IS the one thing you can be sure of, the goal is to figure out how you can use that certainty to your advantage, to modify, transfigure, refashion, and transform your day-to-day being.

—*O, The Oprah Magazine*, **September 2014**

WHAT I KNOW for sure is that the only way to endure the quake is to adjust your stance. You can't avoid the daily tremors. They come with being alive. But I believe these experiences are gifts that force us to step to the right or left in search of a new center of gravity. Don't fight them. Let them help you adjust your footing.

—*What I Know For Sure*, **2014**

WHEN YOU SEE other people who have come through the worst, who have survived what you're going through, it lets you know you can.

—*Makers: Women Who Make America,*
February 26, 2013

HERE'S WHAT I'VE learned: If you don't ask for it, you're not likely to get it.

—*O, The Oprah Magazine*, July 2014

JUST BECAUSE THE phone is ringing doesn't mean I have to respond. I control what I do with my time. We all do, even when it seems out of control. Protect your time. It is your life.

—*What I Know For Sure*, 2014

EVERY FAREWELL OFFERS an opportunity for a new hello. . . . When one road ends, it's time to look ahead in a new direction. And know that as far as your eye can see, the universe can see even farther. That is where we're headed.

—*O, The Oprah Magazine*, May 2015

BRAVERY SHOWS UP in everyday life when people have the courage to live their truth, their vision, and their dreams.

—*O, The Oprah Magazine*, January 2015

EXTEND YOURSELF IN kindness to other human beings wherever you can.

—commencement speech at Harvard University,
May 30, 2013

ALWAYS DO THE right thing—always.... Be excellent. Let excellence be your brand.

—commencement speech at Spelman College,
May 20, 2012

NO DOUBT, WE'RE all more digitally and fiber-optically linked than ever before, but we're apparently losing our real connections.... Listen. Pay attention.... Make the connection.

—*O, The Oprah Magazine*, December 2004

THE ENERGY WE put out in the world is the energy we get back. So, if you want more love in your life, set your intention to be more loving. If you seek kindness, focus your energy on empathy and compassion. Conversely, if you wonder why there are so many angry people in your life, look no further than the resentment you hold in your own heart.

—*The Wisdom of Sundays*, 2017

IT IS POSSIBLE to take your post-traumatic pain and turn that into post-traumatic power and post-traumatic wisdom. I know this for sure that whatever has happened *to* you can also be *for* you if you allow it to be.

—*The Drew Barrymore Show*, April 30, 2021

DON'T UNDERESTIMATE YOUR power. Hate is potent, but so is kindness. And goodness, and grace. Use yours generously.

—*O, The Oprah Magazine*, January 2019

FORGIVE, AND SET yourself free.

—The Wisdom of Sundays, 2017

MY HOPE IS that you will take time out of your life just to give something back to yourself every single day. To connect, to listen, to celebrate yourself and what matters most to you.

—Facebook, March 25, 2021

I BELIEVE THAT everything that is happening to us is happening to lead us to whatever is the greater moment.

—"Oprah's 2020 Vision: Your Life in Focus" tour, January 25, 2020

ONE OF THE most important things I've learned in life is to accept this moment for what it is. Do not spend your energy resisting what is. Get to acceptance as soon as you can and that will allow you to cope with this present moment.

—Facebook, April 29, 2021

BALANCE LIVES IN the present. When you feel the earth moving, bring yourself back to the now. You'll handle whatever shake-up the next moment brings when you get to it. In *this* moment, you're still breathing. In *this* moment, you've survived. In *this* moment, you're finding a way to step onto higher ground.

—*What I Know For Sure*, 2014

TAKE A DEEP breath with me right now and repeat this: Everything is always working out for me. . . . That's my mantra. Make it yours. Everything is always working out for me. Because it is, and it has, and it will continue to be as you forge and discover your own path.

—commencement speech at Colorado College, May 19, 2019

Finding Your Purpose and Leaving a Legacy

EVERYBODY HAS A calling. Your real job in life is to figure out why you are here and get about the business of doing it.

—*The Wisdom of Sundays*, 2017

DON'T EXPECT THE clarity to come all at once, to know your purpose right away.

—**commencement speech at Harvard University,**
May 30, 2013

YOUR LIFE IS your greatest teacher. Every single thing that's happening to you every day: your joys, your sadnesses, your challenges, your worries . . . everything is trying to take you home to yourself. And when you're at home with yourself . . . you are your best.

—**interview at Stanford Graduate School of Business,**
April 16, 2014

KNOWING WHAT YOU *don't* want to do is the best possible place to be . . . because knowing what you don't want to do leads you to figure out what it is you really do want to do.

—interview at Stanford Graduate School of Business,
April 16, 2014

WHAT I KNOW for sure is that the biggest choices begin and end with you—your internal big questions: Who do I want to be in the world?

—commencement speech at Spelman College,
May 20, 2012

MUSIC, LAUGHTER, DANCING (even a party for one), knitting, cooking—finding what naturally soothes you not only regulates your heart and mind, it helps you stay open to the goodness in you and in the world.

—*What Happened to You?*, 2021

The meaning of *wisdom* for me is recognizing the moment when what you *know* aligns perfectly with what you *feel*.

—*The Wisdom of Sundays*, 2017

STRENGTH TIMES STRENGTH times strength equals power. What happened to you can be your power.

—What Happened to You?, 2021

FOR EVERY DREAM, there is automatically going to be resistance. But your sheer will and desire can be stronger than the shadow. You get to decide. You get to declare, I want this, and confront the fear head-on.

—The Path Made Clear: Discovering Your Life's Direction and Purpose, 2019

FEAR IS REAL. We have all experienced it. And it can be a powerful roadblock. The true meaning of courage is to be afraid—and then, with your knees knocking and your heart racing, take the leap anyway.

—The Path Made Clear: Discovering Your Life's Direction and Purpose, 2019

IT'S NOT A myth that some people make their best decisions in the shower—there really is something about the warm spray and lack of distraction that helps crystallize your thoughts.

—*The Path Made Clear: Discovering Your Life's Direction and Purpose,* 2019

THE QUESTION IS, what are you willing to stand for? That question is going to follow you throughout your life. And here's how you answer it. You put your honor where your mouth is. When you give your word, keep it. Show up, do the work, get your hands dirty, and then you will begin to draw strength from the understanding, the true knowing, that history is still being written.

—commencement speech at University of Southern California's Annenberg School for Communication and Journalism, May 11, 2018

You're only on this planet to be you. Not someone else's imitation of you. . . . Your life journey is about learning to become more of who you are and fulfilling the highest, truest expression of yourself as a human being. That's why you're here. You will do that through your work and your art, through your relationships and your love.

—**commencement speech at University of Southern California's Annenberg School for Communication and Journalism, May 11, 2018**

It's such an extraordinary time to be a strong, confident, assured, and, above all else, well woman in the world today.

—**"Oprah's 2020 Vision: Your Life in Focus" tour, February 8, 2020**

THERE WON'T BE a "next Oprah" . . . just like there won't be another Barbara Walters, Aretha Franklin or Whitney Houston. People who make their mark in the way that they made it, that's it.

—*Hollywood Reporter*, December 11, 2013

THERE'S BEEN A lot written lately about midlife depression. Suddenly, midlifers have so many options. Their children are grown and they're asking themselves, "What do I do now? Who am I?" They're looking at the possibility of a second life, at reinventing themselves.

—*USA Today*, March 2, 2008

WHAT I KNOW for sure, sitting high atop the perch of broader perspective at 60: Whether you're trying to create a great conversation or a great life, it's the questions that count. Ask the right questions, and the answers will always reveal themselves.

—*O, The Oprah Magazine*, April 2014

MOST PEOPLE WAIT to assess their legacy until their second or third act of life, when there is time to sit back and reflect. But what if, right now, you began to structure your decisions based on how you want to be remembered, rather than on what you believe you still need to accomplish? What I'm suggesting is that you don't wait until you're sitting on your porch in your rocking chair to evaluate the character of your actions. Ask yourself today, in the middle of your complicated, demanding, chaotic life: What do I want my legacy to be?

—*The Path Made Clear: Discovering Your Life's Direction and Purpose*, 2019

THERE'S A QUICKENING that happens, and your body, your hormones, everything is saying, "Hey, you don't have as much time as you once had— let's get on with it!"

—*Wall Street Journal Magazine*, February 12, 2018

YOUR LEGACY IS made every day.... Every person that you encounter in the space of your life [whom] you impact ... in any way—that will be your legacy.

—interview with former Facebook COO
Sheryl Sandberg, October 2, 2011

Milestones

1954

- Orpah Gail Winfrey (the Biblical "Orpah" was mis-pronounced as "Oprah" and the name stuck) is born in Kosciusko, Mississippi to Vernita Lee and Vernon Winfrey. She remains in Mississippi with her maternal grandmother for the next six years of her life.

1960

- Oprah joins her mother in Milwaukee, Wisconsin. Over the next several years she is sexually abused by members of her family as well as a family friend.

1968

- Vernita sends Oprah to Nashville, Tennessee to live with her father. She gives birth prematurely, and her baby dies shortly afterward.

1971

- Oprah lands her first broadcast job at WVOL radio station in Nashville.

1973

- Oprah becomes the first female television anchor at WLAC-TV in Nashville.

1976

- Oprah moves to Baltimore to co-anchor the six o'clock news for WJZ-TV. She does not get along with her more-established co-anchor and lasts less than a year before she is unceremoniously removed. The station tries her out in different positions and eventually makes her the co-host of the talk show *People Are Talking*.

- Oprah meets Gayle King while working at WJZ-TV. The pair spends a night together during a snowstorm, marking the beginning of a lifelong friendship.

1984

- Oprah makes her Chicago debut as the host of WLS-TV's *AM Chicago*.

1985

- Steven Spielberg's *The Color Purple* is released to widespread acclaim. Oprah is nominated for an Academy Award for Best Supporting Actress for her role as Sofia.

- *AM Chicago* is renamed *The Oprah Winfrey Show*.

1986

- Oprah forms Harpo, her production company.

- *The Oprah Winfrey Show* goes national.

1987

- Oprah wins her first Daytime Emmy Award for Outstanding Talk Show Host; she will go on to win 18 Daytime Emmys and 2 Primetime Emmys as of this book's publication.

1988

- Oprah takes full ownership of *The Oprah Winfrey Show*, becoming the first woman in history to own her own talk show.

1991

- Oprah testifies in front of the United States Senate Judiciary Committee in support of a national database of convicted child abusers. President Clinton will sign "Oprah's Bill" into law two years later, establishing the database.

- Oprah wins Entertainer of the Year at the NAACP Image Awards.

1992

- Oprah becomes engaged to Stedman Graham; the couple remains together but has opted not to marry.

1993

- Oprah's prime-time sit-down with Michael Jackson becomes the most-watched interview ever, with over 90 million viewers. The interview is nominated for a Primetime Emmy for Outstanding Informational Special.

1995

- Oprah is added to the *Forbes'* 400 wealthiest people list with an estimated net worth of $340 million. She is the only Black American on the list that year.

- Oprah is awarded a Peabody Personal Award for her on- and off-air accomplishments.

1996

- Oprah's Book Club is launched. Selection by the book club becomes a sure indicator of commercial success.

- The first episode to feature "Oprah's Favorite Things" airs. The annual show, in which Oprah gives the audience a curated selection of her favorite products for the year, is usually the most-watched show of the season. Items featured on the show routinely receive a large sales boost afterward.

1997

- Oprah forms the Angel Network, which supports charitable organizations and provides grants to non-profits around the world.

1998

- Oprah returns to the screen in an adaptation of Toni Morrison's *Beloved*.

- Oprah receives the Lifetime Achievement Award from the Academy of Television Arts and Sciences (the Emmy Awards).

2000

- *O, The Oprah Magazine* launches and becomes the most successful magazine start-up.

- The NAACP awards Oprah the Spingarn Medal for outstanding achievement by an African American.

2002

- Oprah is the inaugural recipient of the Bob Hope Humanitarian Award from the Academy of Television Arts and Sciences for her contributions to television and radio.

2003

- Oprah becomes the first female Black American billionaire listed in *Forbes'* annual ranking.

2004

- Oprah travels to South Africa to film *Oprah's Christmas Kindness*, a show that brings awareness to children affected by poverty and AIDs. Viewers donate over $7 million to the Angel Network in response. Oprah stays with former South African president Nelson Mandela, where she forms the idea to create a school in South Africa for girls.

2005

- *Forbes* names Oprah the world's most powerful celebrity. She will again be #1 in 2007, 2008, 2010, and 2013.

- The NAACP Image Awards inducts her into its Hall of Fame.

2006

- Oprah launches a new radio station, Oprah Radio, in partnership with XM Satellite Radio. Her contract is worth a reported $55 million for three years.

2007

- The Oprah Winfrey Leadership Academy for Girls opens in South Africa. Controversy erupts when several students accuse a dorm matron of physical and sexual abuse. Oprah initiates an independent investigation and flies to South Africa to speak to the students and their parents directly. The dorm matron is eventually acquitted, but Oprah maintains that she believes the girls. Her swift and decisive handling of the incident wins praise by local papers and experts dealing in sexual abuse.

- Oprah endorses Barack Obama in the 2008 Democratic presidential primary, marking her first official political endorsement.

2008

- Together with Discovery Communications, Oprah creates OWN: The Oprah Winfrey Network. The initial launch date is 2009, but is pushed back to 2011.

- In her role as chairwoman of Harpo, the *Hollywood Reporter* names her the most powerful woman in entertainment.

2009

- Oprah announces that the 25th season of *The Oprah Winfrey Show* (airing 2010–2011) will be its last.

2010

- Oprah is honored by the Kennedy Center for contributions to media.

2011

- OWN launches in January. An estimated 505,000 viewers tune in during its first week.

- Oprah receives the Jean Hersholt Humanitarian Award from the Academy of Motion Pictures.

- OWN CEO Christina Norman is replaced by Discovery executive Peter Ligouri in May after the network fails to gain new viewership.

- The last episode of *The Oprah Winfrey Show* airs on May 25. The episode is watched by an estimated 16.4 million viewers.

- Oprah takes over as CEO and chief creative officer of OWN in July.

2012

- OWN lays off 20 percent of its workforce and undergoes further restructuring.

- Tyler Perry enters into a partnership with OWN, creating two scripted shows for the network. Perry's original shows become OWN's most consistently watched.

2013

- OWN reports that it is profitable for the first time since the channel launched.

- Oprah returns to the big screen with a role in Lee Daniels' *The Butler*. She is nominated for several awards, including an NAACP Image Award, BAFTA Award, and SAG award.

- Oprah is awarded the Presidential Medal of Freedom.

2014

- *Forbes* ranks Oprah the 14th most powerful woman in the world.

- Oprah appears in Ava DuVernay's *Selma*. In her role as an executive producer, she is nominated for an Academy Award for Best Picture, among other awards.

2015

- OWN reports four years of positive viewership growth. Perry's shows for OWN routinely draw several million viewers.

- Oprah buys a 10 percent ownership stake in Weight Watchers that includes a seat on its board; its stock price soars in the immediate aftermath.

2016

- CNN Money reports a surprise $11 million quarterly loss for Weight Watchers, raising questions about the power of Oprah's influence.

- Oprah wins a Tony Award for Best Musical Revival for her role as co-producer of *The Color Purple*.

- Oprah returns to scripted television with OWN's drama *Greenleaf*.

- Oprah endorses Hillary Clinton for president.

- The Harpo Studios complex in Chicago is demolished, closing that chapter in Oprah's life.

2017

- *Food, Health, and Happiness*, a cookbook featuring some of Oprah's most cherished recipes, and *The Wisdom of Sundays*, a collection of conversations from OWN's Emmy-winning TV show *Super Soul Sunday*, are published.

2018

- Oprah receives the Cecil B. DeMille Award for outstanding contributions to the world of entertainment from The Hollywood Foreign Press Association (the Golden Globes).

- The National Museum of African American History and Culture opens a special exhibit on Oprah and her cultural influence.

- Oprah stars as Mrs. Which in the film adaptation of *A Wrinkle in Time*.

2019

- *The Path Made Clear*, Oprah's personal guide to living life to the fullest, is published.

- Oprah launches *Oprah's Super Soul*, a podcast featuring conversations from her *Super Soul Sunday* series and exclusive new interviews.

2020

- Oprah goes on her "Oprah's 2020 Vision: Your Life in Focus" tour, which features special guests such as Michelle Obama, Lady Gaga, and Tina Fey.

- Oprah donates over $10 million to support those impacted by the COVID-19 pandemic.

- Oprah sells the majority of her OWN shares to Discovery, reducing her stake to just 5 percent of the network. Oprah retains the titles of CEO and Chief Creative Officer of OWN.

2021

- Oprah's interview with Prince Harry and Meghan Markle, the Duke and Duchess of Sussex, airs on March 8. The special is watched by an estimated 17 million viewers and is nominated for a Primetime Emmy.

- *What Happened to You?*, a book on trauma and healing co-authored by Oprah and psychiatrist Bruce D. Perry, is published.

2022

- *Sidney*, a Sidney Poitier documentary produced by Oprah, airs on Apple TV on September 23.

Acknowledgments

We would like to thank Henry Begler, Johnna Caboz, Kelsey Dame, Amanda Gibson, Paige Gilberg, Mira Green, Eva Lopez, Yola Mzizi, Erin Rosenberg, Suzanne Sonnier, Lily Walker, and Joy Zhao for their invaluable contributions to the preparation of this manuscript.